THE ROAD TO HELL

GRAHAM WATSON

THE ROAD TO HELL

7/379332

SPRINGFIELD BOOKS LIMITED

Published by Springfield Books Limited,
Norman Road, Denby Dale, Huddersfield
HD8 8TH, West Yorkshire, England

First edition 1992

British Library Cataloguing in Publication Data
Watson, Graham
  Road to Hell
  I Title
  796.6

ISBN 1 85688 022 2

Edited: Whiteline Publishing Services
Design: Chris Hand, Design for Print
Typesetting: Selwood Systems, Midsomer Norton
Printed and bound in Hong Kong by Colorcraft Ltd

CONTENTS

FOREWORD

by Sean Kelly

The biggest smile he's ever worn; Sean Kelly after his first Lombardy win in 1983

The big classics appeal to me because of their history, and because I have competed in them so often. Even for me there is magic in them, because I know that these races were won by all the great bike riders of the past, and that their appeal to the public has never ceased. I shall never forget the first time I raced in the classics. I was nervous of climbs like the Kwaremont and Mur de Grammont in Flanders, and of the speeds at which we raced over the cobblestones of Paris–Roubaix – and I had to learn quickly. In fact my first classic was the 1977 Milan–San Remo where 360 riders took part. Riding in such a big peloton was scary at the time and you are presented with so many new kinds of problems.

The classics have a special meaning for me because of the difficulties, the bad weather, the hardness of the racing and the timing. It's possible for me to prepare myself for the Spring Classics. I can train for them, and then from mid-March to the end of April I can look forward to arriving in San Remo, riding in Flanders and pedalling into Roubaix or Liège at the end of a hard day. Then of course there is the Tour of Lombardy, another favourite of mine, to round the season off with in October. This classic provides riders with the best chance to retrieve a bad season or make a great season out of an ordinary one.

What really brought home their importance to me was the time when I missed the classics for a couple of seasons due to injury, and it was difficult to sit and watch without pangs of pain and anguish at seeing the races on TV. Many of my personal memories are contained in this book, especially my wins in the 1983 Tour of

Lombardy and the 1984 Paris–Roubaix. These were two of my early classics victories; they mean a lot to me, and gave me great satisfaction and confidence. I regret not having won the Tour of Flanders, having been second three times – that's cycling.

I am glad Graham Watson has produced The Road to Hell, as he is always there with his camera at the most important moments, and I can see the results in the papers and magazines. He captures the spirit and the images of the classics, and like the rider he has to endure the bad weather, the *pavé*, the dust and the motor traffic. His work is a credit both to his profession and to himself, and it will live on as a record of the great races and the great riders.

Kelly during the 1988 Paris–Roubaix

INTRODUCTION

One day in the spring of 1980 completely changed my whole way of life. It was a warm sunny afternoon, and I'd just arrived on a cobbled track near the village of Gruson, having cycled all the way from Calais with the intention of seeing the Paris–Roubaix cycling classic. It had been a long eight-hour ride to this spot, battering into a stiff headwind all the way, not knowing if I'd make it in time to see the race – not even knowing if I'd find the race! My motive for making the trip had been the excitement of seeing the previous weekend's Tour of Flanders, and that trip had in turn been motivated by having seen the Tour de France for two summers running and wanting to see more. But as exciting as those previous adventures had been, they were to pale into insignificance compared with this one – for I was

The winning escape of Marc Madiot (left) in 1991, is captured in the same spot that I'd first seen Paris–Roubaix eleven years earlier where my shot had been blocked by Henri Besson's motorbike

actually riding my bike to see the most famous one-day bike race in the world.

Little did I know that this was the very kind of challenge I was going to continue repeating over the next decade and more, as I followed the great one-day classics and tours all over Europe. That ride to see Paris–Roubaix holds so much significance because it sealed my addiction to cycle racing in a way no previous race ever had – not even the Tour de France. One man in particular shared the responsibility for fuelling that addiction, for he'd already caught my eye in the Tour of Flanders: Francesco Moser. Racing so proudly in front on all the major hills and landmarks in the Belgian classic, Moser was for me elegance personified – his courage endless, his determination absolute. I thought a lot about my hero as I rode to see Paris–Roubaix, for it was he that was drawing me across the patchwork landscape of the Pas-de-Calais that afternoon to see the *pavé* of the 'Hell of the North'.

I'd already read sufficiently well about him to know his pedigree, and of course to know he'd already won Paris–Roubaix twice. But I never dreamt I'd see him win it again with my own eyes, which is exactly what happened on this Sunday afternoon in northern France. I'd found my way from the seaport, via the city of Lille, to arrive on this cobbled track with just 20 minutes to spare before the race was due to arrive, having been blown towards Roubaix by the same wind that had slowed me down. Even as I arrived, the track was already vibrating with the pressure from the press and officials' cars pounding over it; the ground literally shook beneath my feet. And along its feathered edges I waited – we all waited, thousands of us growing ever more excited at the imminent arrival of the race.

In those days I knew no French whatsoever, and certainly no Flemish, so I had no idea where the race was, or who was leading it. Nor did I care. I only felt exuberance at fulfilling my adventure of seeing Paris–Roubaix. More cars materialised, showering my camera with particles of white dirt. I refocused once again, anxious at the thought of missing this first-ever shot. Then came motorbikes, dozens of them, followed by another car, then another swarm of motorbikes, and then Moser. I'd spotted his distinctive jersey immediately, even amongst the blinding confusion of motorbikes, cars and dust. But even before that I'd spotted his hawk-like nose, perched predaciously over his handlebars.

My hero blasted by at over 30 miles per hour, his figure merely a fleeting glimpse amongst the motorbikes and dust that so annoyingly engulfed him. I was dazed. It was over so quickly, and my shot had been ruined by those damn motorbikes. Yet I will never forget that moment when Moser raced along the dirt edges of the track just feet from where I stood, his Italian champion's tricolour jersey so startling in the blinding sunlight. It's an image I still remember so lovingly today – an image still so clear in my mind despite all the incredible memories I've amassed since that afternoon in the Pas-de-Calais. From that moment on, I was hooked on cycle racing, and in particular one-day racing, to the point where I wanted to see every classic in the world. But I wanted to see it, not from the roadside, but from the pillion seat of a motorbike, like one of those that had so selfishly obscured my view that afternoon.

Since then I've realised my ambitions many times over – with the same degree of passion and enthusiasm that brought me to see my first Paris–Roubaix. And whereas it was Moser then, it is now Sean Kelly, or Marc Madiot, or Steve Bauer, that I photograph from that same spot near Gruson, shooting them from a motorbike to get those very photos I was denied so many years ago. Twelve years on, it is not just Paris–Roubaix that commands my affection, for now all the great classics thrill me in some way or another, just as I expected they would do if I ever got to see them. The Tour of Flanders, Ghent–Wevelgem, Milan–San Remo, Liège–Bastogne–Liège, and the Tour of Lombardy each have a distinct identity and character, yet they are for ever bound together in cycling folklore by the reputations their histories have created.

Witnessing a classic is like travelling back in time, because there is so much that remains miraculously unchanged by modern ways. One can see today's 'stars' assault an obstacle such as the Muur van Geraardsbergen, sensing that their desperate struggle is a living playback of their predecessors' efforts half a century ago. Only their rewards have changed, while the barbaric cobblestones of the Wallers-Arenberg forest illustrate with cruel clarity that cycling is still one of the toughest sports of all. The awesome reputation of the classics is due in large part to the courage of the men that race in them – men like Leon Houa of Belgium, who won that first-ever Liège–Bastogne–Liège in 1892; or the Flemish cyclist Achiel Buysse, who was the first to win three Tours of Flanders; or Fred de Bruyne, who was the first cyclist to win the four biggest classics: Milan–San Remo, Tour of Flanders, Paris–Roubaix and Liège–Bastogne–Liège.

My trusted 'motard' Patrice, whose skills have played a major role in my own success

Eddy Planckaert, photographed in full cry on the Muur Van Geraardsbergen in the 1990 Omloop Het Volk

Today's victors take their lead from a man whose achievements did more for cycling than anybody else: Eddy Merckx. Merckx came into the sport at a time when Belgium was the dominant cycling nation, at a time when Belgian races struck fear into others. Merckx superseded anything his own predecessors – Rik Van Steenbergen or Rik Van Looy – had done in the classics and his supporters were over the moon with his 32 classic victories. Nowadays, Belgium is still a dominant force in cycling, and a visit to this country more than any other will show why the cycling classics are so absorbing. If you spend time in some cosy roadside café whilst waiting for a race such as the season-opening Omloop Het Volk, then you'll be watching and listening to a nation's love affair with the bicycle and with the rugged men who've instilled so much pride in these loyal fans. To mingle with the old men of Flanders is to learn about the classics – the way they used to be raced, the way they used to be won, the way they should be won.

These trips down memory lane can be made at any great race, and in any cycling-mad country. But Belgium is special because of its glorious history in the classics, and of course because it spawned Eddy Merckx. It's impossible to go to any race in Europe without being made vividly aware of Merckx's role in shaping the reputation of the classics we know today. When, in the 1990 Liège-Bastogne-Liège, I peer through my camera lens at Eric Van Lancker's attack on the Côte des Forges, I find myself totally absorbed by the Belgian's motivation, and by the sight of his fleeing form as he chases towards Liège. But as if in a 15-year-old playback, I find myself wondering if this is what it was like when Merckx was winning his fifth Liège-Bastogne-Liège.

In the dozen years since I saw Moser in the Paris-Roubaix, my sights have broadened somewhat. Inspired by that adventure in northern France, I travelled further afield: to Holland, to southern Belgium, to southern France, to Spain – and of course to Moser's own country, Italy, where just one year after that Paris-Roubaix I saw my first Milan–San Remo. Amid the drama of these cut-and-thrust races, other heroes entered the fray: Eric Vanderaerden, Phil Anderson, Claude Criquielion, Steve Bauer and Eddy Planckaert; Jan Raas and Hennie Kuiper too. But one man in particular stood out from the rest, and he became a hero every bit as much as Moser: Sean Kelly.

To travel for nine months of the year, through excitement and trauma, through successes and setbacks, you need to develop a motivation that will launch you from one race to the next. Kelly did this for me – did it from the moment I saw him win his first classic in 1983, in Italy, just a few feet ahead of Moser. As I saw him wheel back down the finishing straight that day, his face lit from cheek to cheek with the broadest smile, the significance of that first win suddenly dawned on me. For here was not a Frenchman, a Belgian or an Italian who had won: an English-speaking cyclist had won a classic, and was to win many more. In the years that followed that first victory, Kelly wove his own name into the history of the classics, doing it in such a thorough way that it will be some time before a successor is found. His third victory in the Tour of Lombardy, coming eight years after his first, brought the legend of Sean Kelly full-circle; and being there brought my classics adventure full-circle too.

Since Kelly's victory in Lombardy in 1983, the classics have changed somewhat – or at least they've been redefined in the light of the sport's changing structure and values. New races have come along, hosted by countries that never before had a 'classic' to host. Although brought in as a means of opening up professional cycling to a wider audience, these new races have in fact devalued the real meaning of a classic to the point where only a mere handful of races can now be justifiably termed as such. Five such races form the basis of this book, and it's no coincidence that the new 'classics' are completely absent. Milan–San Remo, Tour of Flanders, Paris–Roubaix, Liège-Bastogne-Liège and Tour of Lombardy are now what are termed 'monuments' in cycling – untouchable. No matter which direction the sport goes from here, no amount of political, material or commercial influence will ever dilute the glorious heritage of these great races.

To be a photographer of the one-day classics is to be an observer of a fight to the death. For a one-day race is a compelling drama about winning – and only winning. In a stage race every day brings another dimension, another chance for a cyclist to improve his standing, but in a classic there's no second chance. Nobody cares who comes second. The fight to win is what makes the racing so special, and so exciting to rider, spectator and photographer alike. For those who cannot win, the fight resembles a living hell, and this too is an essential ingredient of the attraction to classic one-day racing. The races are raw, brittle and merciless, and the courses they are raced over utterly terrifying. The men that race in them are heroes, loved and adored by spectators all across Europe in a very different way from stage-race cyclists.

It's not for nothing that the months of March, April and October mean so much to me, for it is then that the classics take place. I've been especially privileged to be a part of these great races, and I've often needed special favours from certain people in order to be there; access to these races as a photographer is never guaranteed, and certainly not for an Englishman working in a sport so continental. In particular, Fons Märien has been of enormous help to me in his role within the syndicate of Belgian sports photographers, often turning a blind eye to officialdom in order to accommodate my wishes to follow the prestigious Belgian classics on a motorbike. And my affection for Belgium, and for the Belgian classics, wouldn't have been realised without the hospitality shown to me over the years by Piet and Linda Van Belle.

I owe a lot to the performance of Francesco Moser that April afternoon in 1980, and owe a lot as well to the ambitions of those men who still try so hard to emulate the Italian's flair and determination. They are the reason why I hope my love affair with the classics will go on for some considerable time. For as long as there are heroes, I want to be there to photograph them – to share their battles in trying to win a classic.

CLAUDIO CHIAPPUCCI

19 March 1991: Milan–San Remo

The haul up to Capo Mele was hurting them all now, the pouring rain having taken its toll of the eleven-man breakaway group that had been away for more than 100 kilometres. And the brave escapers were well into the sights of the big peloton, spread like hungry wolves along the wide, wet sea road. The escapers knew this: one by one they all looked round, all, except Claudio Chiappucci. Instead, he accelerated to rid his group of all but the most tenacious attackers, then attacked again on the Capo Berta, with the peloton still in sight behind. It seemed a forlorn hope on the part of the Carrera rider – a desperate move,

even though Rolf Sörensen had joined Chiappucci's acceleration.

The peloton eased as it caught the latest casualties of Chiappucci's forcefulness, allowing the two fugitives a further chance to regain their advantage. There seemed little difference in their strengths, the Italian was taking longer pulls on the uphill sections; Sörensen contributed willingly by burying himself on the flats. The Cipressa was drawing near, the Poggio came soon after that, and the peloton was just 50 seconds behind. Could they survive? They set about it in a grand manner that deserved success, whatever fate awaited them by the end of the day.

The Cipressa's summit passed by with their lead up to one minute and 30 seconds. The tricky descent gained them another ten seconds, and they attacked the ten-kilometre flat to the Poggio's base with the virtual assurance that one of them would win the opening grand classic of the season. As the Poggio drew ever closer I detected a growing awareness on the part of Chiappucci that he was close to emulating Gianni Bugno's speculative win the previous year, for his eyes sparkled in the light of my flashgun as it sought out the leaders in the decreasing light. Sörensen seemed less sparkling, and I had made my decision in the light of the Poggio's influence in the race. As soon as they hit the initial ascent from the sea road, Chiappucci attacked, losing Sörensen immediately. Now only eight kilometres separated the unsung hero of Italian cycling from another headline-catching performance.

The powerhouse stormed up the climb, his face contorted with the efforts of succeeding in his three-and-a-half-hour escape, and it was impossible not to feel moved by his efforts. For a few brief seconds he was directly behind the motorbike as I framed him in flat-out style approaching the summit; we then followed him all the way to the bottom, greatly impressed by his courageous climbing, and now by his skilful descending. By the time the last 800 metres of this long race had been reached, he had a comfortable advantage. At the finish Chiappucci came home to a hero's welcome, with the previously uncertain *tifosi* now moved to delirium. An Italian had won the Milan–San Remo for the second year in succession.

A bird's-eye view of the 1989 start which runs along the side of Il Duomo

16

MILAN–SAN REMO

'La Gazzetta! La Gazzetta!' The crowd gathered eagerly around the portly man, hurriedly exchanging their *lire* for a copy of the newspaper whose pink-coloured pages contained the riders' line-up for Milan–San Remo, and the route the race would take to its finish on the Mediterranean coast. It's the third weekend in March, and the milling crowds beside the *Piazza Duomo* are jostling for a glimpse of their heroes – the men who will shortly be setting off to do battle in the Primavera, the first great one-day classic of the season. The dress is a mixture of chic Milanese – velvet-collared cashmere overcoats and freshly pressed brown trousers – and that of the die-hard cycling enthusiasts, decked out in trade jerseys from the present decade or from three decades past.

Faded jerseys are everywhere to be seen – Molteni, Bianchi, Brooklyn, Magniflex, Salvarani – all of them worn by men in their fifties or sixties, for whom this gathering acts as a glorious pageant to some past Milan–San Remo in which a Merckx, a Gimondi, a De Vlaeminck, even a Coppi, could be remembered racing to victory in those very same colours. The old men stand talking avidly with each other, having ridden in from all parts of the city to experience once again the special atmosphere of Milan–San Remo. For most of them the race will go out of sight when the peloton moves out of the city and onto the misty plains of Lombardy, while the more adventurous ones will use four-wheeled transport to see the race as often as ten times during the day, having conveniently left their cars at some nearby spot in the city.

A walk amongst the crowds brings these *tifosi* into poignant contact with their heroes, for the stars of yesterday are to be found making their own entrance in the piazza. Felice Gimondi, Gianni Motta, Giuseppe Saronni and Francesco Moser – especially Moser – are as much a part of the race today as they were in their glory days. Even Gino Bartali – the oldest living winner of a Giro d'Italia, and a man who won Milan–San Remo four times between 1939 and 1950 – can be seen holding conversations with fans young and old, who listen awe-struck as the great old man recalls his legendary battles in the race with the late Fausto Coppi. Today's stars are harder to sight, hidden as they are in their team cars, a refuge from the autograph hunters who will find no sympathy here – not on a day as important as this.

Suddenly an official's whistle can be heard from somewhere in the crowd. Its piercing effect on the masses becomes very obvious as journalists and race followers begin to search for their cars spread up to a kilometre down the street. There's no such panic for the photographers aboard their motorbikes, for we will be part of the peloton that is about to make its exit from the piazza, part of the massive entourage that epitomises the might and glamour of this famous race. The riders begin to emerge from the sanctuary of their cars; mechanics rush across in response to some last-minute problem with a slipping gear lever or loose saddle; the *tifosi* close in for a last-chance photograph at the side of their chosen icon before landing an enthusiastic slap on his back.

There's joy and chaos at the start of Milan–San Remo every year: joy because it heralds the true start of another season of racing; chaos because we're back in Italy, and at a race where the pressure is never greater. It's the first great meeting of the season for all the riders, following on from training races in Spain, France and Sicily, and the traditional twinned weeks of Paris–Nice and Tirreno–Adriatico – races where teams and riders try so hard to avoid each other, scared to expose their form before the right moment. And the right moment is Milan–San Remo – for so important is a good performance in the *Primavera* that the hype and pressure surrounding this first classic will never be equalled, not even in the ensuing classics of the north. There is an awful disquiet hovering over the riders as they line up below the impressive cathedral.

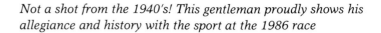

Because of the traffic chaos of a Saturday morning in Milan, a neutralised stretch of road will take the race to its official start three kilometres away, but not before buses, taxis, cars and pedestrians are halted in grand style. Driving beside the giant peloton, we spend these gentle moments greeting friendly faces not encountered since last autumn, familiarising ourselves with their new colours while taking critical note of their glistening muscles: will he do well today?

The race pauses alongside a filthy canal, for just a minute or two – time enough for riders to remove or put on items of clothing; time too for a communal halt for nature. On the far side of the canal, a stream of cyclists is already making its way on a parallel route to the race, while behind us the cycling *tifosi* are readying themselves for a lung-bursting dash behind the race; they've made it this far, so why not a few more kilometres at full race pace?

Up ahead the organiser, Torriani, waves his red flag from his Lancia's sunroof, and the race pulls away from its official start, leaving great streams of urine in the street, the peloton having flushed itself of several hundred cappuccini consumed at cafés behind the cathedral. Seeing Vincenza Torriani serves as a reminder of the adventures to come later in the day as the race reaches its summit along the *capi* of the Mediterranean coast. But that is seven hours away, and Torriani won't be confronted until the last hour of the race, having probably enjoyed a three-course lunch taken somewhere along the motorway route to the sea.

Immediately the race winds up to 50 kilometres per hour, disgorging all but the hardiest of *tifosi* from its slipstream. Yet still one or two remain, floating along in the dangerous convoy of team cars spread out behind the line of riders. Every time the pace slows, these passionate fans will creep slowly back into the peloton before losing their places again as the race accelerates once more. Ultimately, the *carabinieri* must do their job, physically pulling the errant cyclists to a halt just long enough to break their last contact with the

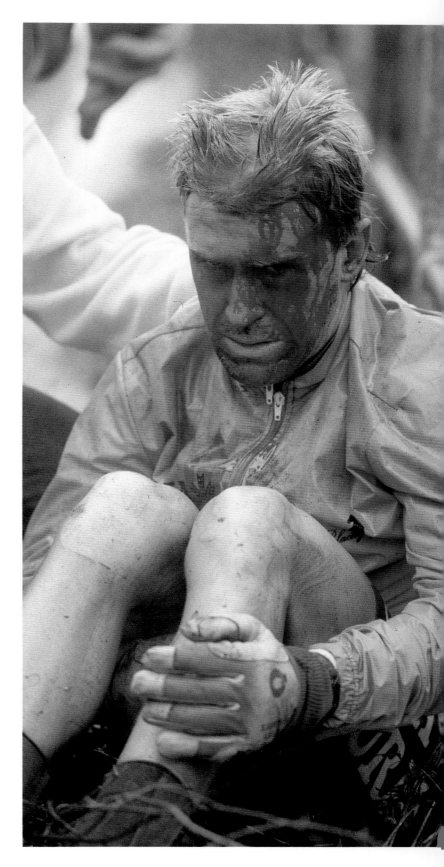

professionals. Their next rendezvous with the *Primavera* will be in five hours time, courtesy of RAI television. The race rumbles on, its speed alternating between 50 and 60 kilometres per hour at regular intervals, exciting the onlookers waiting at every road junction along the way, and sending fear into the hearts of all those first-year professionals riding in this, their first-ever one-day classic.

Today the riders of Chateau d'Ax are keeping the pace high, their movements eyed so suspiciously by the teams of Panasonic, PDM and Buckler – Dutchmen to the core who normally adopt this posture in the race. The race suddenly winds up. Perhaps one of those Dutchmen has got into that front line, stirring things up to tease the 'soft' Italians – no doubt expecting, as nearly everyone else did, that the home riders would disappear from the scene when it mattered most. After all they've only won Milan–San Remo five times in the last 20 years. Nobody at this point knows how the face of world cycling is to change almost by virtue of today's result.

We were now driving just behind the group at the request of Signor Albani, the race *commissaire*, who was nervous of an imminent passage through an intersection up ahead. He was right too, for a sudden twitch in the strung-out field left a clutch of riders lying in the road. I braced myself for work.

The crash had happened more than three-quarters of the way down the 500-metre line, and it seemed ages before we drew up to where the crash victims lay. There seemed to be just three of them, sprawled in various states in the road. One poor guy had ridden straight into a metal 'keep right' sign, and now lay writhing in agony from his wounds. The metal post lay flattened 20 feet away, ripped from its cemented foundations by the speed and impact with which the RMO rider had hit. I shuddered at this sight, yet still had the cruel wish to record the scene, grateful that the victim seemed not badly hurt.

The Chateau d'Ax riders were still on the front, still winding things up at over 50 kilometres per hour. I

Buckler riders abandon ship and scuttle for their team bus after quitting the 1990 race

wanted to be behind the race as it encountered a gradual change in direction, wiggling over a couple of very short undulations before dropping into the Po valley.
With experience one can sense things happening in a race before they actually do, and today something about the pace, the manner in which the peloton was moving along, stirred my instincts; something was happening now, and before my very eyes the compacted group began to break up. First there was a regroupment – one of many already made in the constant changing of pace – then an acceleration from a group of riders at the front. Instantly the pace increased again, just as it had done a dozen times already this morning, and this time seemed no different from the others. But now there was something different: a big hole was developing in the very heart of the race, and from where I stood, up on the pedals behind Patrice, I could see that the peloton was coming apart.

As each metre flew by, so the gaps continued to grow as the pace increased. Experience told me in an instant who was in the back half of this momentous split. I spotted the familiar backs of riders left in the last section of the field: Kelly, Fignon, Criquielion; they'd just been chatting away. So too had Vanderaerden, Van Hooydonck and LeMond, left idling at the back while a score of attackers at the front realised the potential in the changing wind. Scenes like this are a regular feature of big-time professional racing, and I fully expected the gaps to close immediately. Kelly seemed to be the key to all of this; other riders, bewildered by this deviation from the usual Milan–San Remo pattern, looked around to see what was being done about this minor irritation in their day. Then they looked to Kelly, the grand old master of one-day racing.

At first the Irishman seemed unconcerned, no doubt confident of his PDM team's influence in the race: 'Yes,

Wet conditions, caused by melting snow on the Turchino Pass, turned these riders' faces black and gave the photographers a field day. 1986 saw Luciano Rabottini lead Charly Mottet and Marc Seargent to the summit.

they'll sort it out for me', he seemed to be thinking. But when nothing had happened after a few more minutes, Kelly grew anxious, his grey-haired upright head twitching left and right, up and down, scanning the damage now 200 metres up ahead. He conferred with Fignon, then with his old friend Criquielion: 'We'd better do something'. They started to ride alarmed by the gap between them and the group in front. I too could see

that group easily, and the two other groups even further ahead; I felt Kelly hadn't seen this and couldn't appreciate the true implications. To complicate things, very few of Kelly's PDM team or Fignon's team-mates were close by.

I watched curiously as Kelly's not-so-heroic team tried to organise themselves. From our radio it seemed the teams of Del Tongo, Ariostea and Chateau d'Ax had

7/379332

21

Going for it: Maurizio Fondriest's counter-attack on the Cipressa hill in 1990, with Jean-Claude Colotti hanging on . . .

. . . which resulted in this elite chasing group led by Moreno Argentin, Gilles Delion and Jesper Skibby

Chiappucci and Sörensen approach the Poggio hill in 1991

all of their riders in the front groups that were on the verge of joining forces – and that teams such as RMO, Helvetia and 7-Eleven had just their star riders up there. Most problematical for the likes of Kelly and Fignon was that the original attackers seemed to be made up of *domestiques*, many from their own two teams. It had a disastrous effect on the stars' ability to chase. Slowly the two rear groups merged now, and for a moment it seemed things would soon settle down. But instead of continuing the chase, the stars took stock of their new situation, calculating whether they needed to sap more energy so early in the race. We'd barely covered 25 kilometres of this 294-kilometre race!

In the ensuing calm after the first big chase, the gap had grown again to more than 400 metres, and the front group could now only be seen as a dark mass on the horizon. The wide road between was devoid of anything. No humans, no cyclists – not one single car or motorbike. It was an impressive situation, and a few minutes later we sped through the town of Pavia with the normally enthusiastic occupants almost silenced by what they'd heard – and now seen – of this year's Milan–San Remo. The large slabs of stone that paved the main street rattled beneath us as the convoy of about 100 cyclists, 20 motorbikes, nearly 50 team cars and an armada of officials' cars hurtled through town at 60 kilometres per hour. Up ahead, the front group must have been doing 60 as well, for we had made no apparent gains by the time we reached the clear road from Pavia.

Up until now, Signor Albani had kept everyone behind the chasers, but now he signalled that it was safe for us to go through – but one by one, and with no photography. True to our word, we sped across the ever-widening gap. I was keen to see who the strong men were in this stupendous move in the race, keen to record the attack in case – just in case – they failed in their audacious plan. There were perhaps 100 men in that group as well, including most of Gianni Bugno's Chateau d'Ax team that was the most energetic at the front. On

hearing the build-up of motorbikes behind their group, some of the riders at the back twisted round in their saddles to look at the entourage – a sure sign their attack was showing good promise.

The radio continued its string of time checks during the next 15 minutes that summed up the situation. When we'd gone across to the leaders, the gap had been barely half a kilometre or 40 seconds: now, still only 40 kilometres into the seven-hour race, that lead had trebled, to the extent that it would take a complete collapse of effort by the front group for them to lose their advantage. However, I was still perplexed: this wasn't meant to happen in Milan–San Remo, and how could virtually all of the race favourites be left behind? It seemed unfair. I tried to think of the implications of photographing this small peloton all the way to San Remo, as the spectacle of a full peloton massing its armies along the coast road became a fast-diminishing hope.

Gone too would be that congested thrash up the Turchino Pass, the rapid descent to Voltri, the incessant attacks on the *capi* taking the race onto the Cipressa. What was there left for us to do? We'd even lost the calamitous braking of a bunched peloton through the towns before the Turchino; there'd be no more crashes today.

Such was the pace that the race arrived at the village of Ovada more than one hour ahead of schedule with only 119 kilometres covered. Only now did the leaders throttle back from their fast pace, content to have built a fine three-minute lead over the race favourites: I took heart in this slowdown, hoping that the remainder of the race might see the chasers coming back into the reckoning, picturing a make-believe scene on the Poggio when the breakaways were passed by Kelly, Fignon and LeMond. What a finale that would be!

We were now on the Turchino itself – a gradual winding ascent through the hills of Liguria. The progress of this unusual Milan–San Remo was watched by hundreds of spectators who'd parked their cars on the

The fourth of Argentin's attacks on the Poggio in 1992 . . . which seemed certain to secure his victory, until Sean Kelly's brilliant response in the eleventh hour meant his efforts were in vain

autostrada that followed its own winding route, tunnelling through the hills and down to the sea. It must have looked odd, this unlikely pursuit.

I did my best to capture some interesting pictures of the climb, but the familiar explosive images of the Turchino were not there now; the 100 leaders had the race already under control. We passed through the small tunnel at the summit, our ears ringing with the cries of Bugno! Fondriest! Argentin! At least the *tifosi* were happy now. I stopped Patrice halfway down the descent, wanting to do a visual check on the chasers' movements. There were still about 150 kilometres to complete from here to the Poggio, but I believed that if the chasers hadn't begun closing the gap by now, the race was as good as over from their perspective. Two minutes passed, then two-and-a-half, and finally three minutes had gone when we at last could see the first rider careering down through the hairpins above the bend where we waited. Soon the chasers were streaming past us, lining themselves up for the sharp left-hand bend where we watched.

We followed them down to Voltri, not sure whether the speed they'd reached on the long descent would be maintained along the coast road. At first there was some action at the front, with some riders trying one last time to motivate the group into chasing hard again. But then our radio crackled into life once more, drawing a final curtain over this last-chance effort; they had been timed onto the sea-front four-and-a-half minutes behind the Italian-led breakaway. I was angry now, fearing this Milan–San Remo had been robbed of its credibility – angry too that I would be going home without a decent picture stock of the big names. I recalled past editions of the race when this cruise along the seaside had endowed my portfolio with so many exciting images of the stars, riding at an impressive cadence towards the crux of the race.

Today those same stars were just shadows of their former immortality – ordinary cyclists devoid of their desire to succeed. I became depressed at this apathy on such a great occasion. Was this the way the sport was going now? I clung to the hope that something might still shake this group to chase, dejected anyway at the steady yet monotonous progress the front group was making with more than two hours still to the Cipressa. I trailed alongside riders such as Kelly and Martin Earley, trying to read their minds as to what they might yet conjure up for us, even swapping brief conversation with these two Irishmen in an attempt to grasp their reaction to this extraordinary race. But like Fignon, like Criquielion –like a dozen other 'names' – their faces revealed nothing but a hint of growing acceptance of their fate today; I expected all of them to stop at the first feeding station in Savona, now just a few kilometres away. However they continued at a sedate pace.

Eventually the Buckler team pulled in, and I rushed to get shots of Vanderaerden and Van Hooydonck for a Flemish newspaper I was working for, catching their emotions as they loosened their front wheels in preparation for a hurried dash into their transport; their reluctance to be humiliated in their national press was clear to see.

By now I'd had enough, and we drove away at high speed, finally discarding any interest in the idlers; we'd have to make do with what was left of the race ahead. Even travelling at 80 kilometres per hour, it took a massive ten minutes to catch up with the leading bunch. By which time my disappointment had increased twofold, as we had passed so many favourite locations of mine that had shown the true sparkle of Milan–San Remo in the past – especially the colour-drenched peloton in a perfect wedding with the deep-blue Mediterranean.

When we did get to the leaders, it was with the knowledge that this was the race. Nothing that had happened before now was of any importance; I simply had to put out of my mind the disillusion of the first four hours, nothing less would do. Besides, the line-up here wasn't so bad: Sörensen, Argentin, Fondriest, Bugno, Gölz, Baffi, Delion – not the very best in the world, but

This shot of Rolf Gölz in 1990 was taken very late in the race . . .

perhaps some of the best. I got on with the job in hand, absorbing the mood of this mini-peloton and the pattern of its riding in order to regain my 'touch'. Pretty soon the second feed would be upon us, and the racing would grow intense with the Capo Mele, the first of the series of small hills now being encountered by the leaders.

It was the Ariostea team that took control, steaming through the feeding station at Alassio with its three strongmen at the front – Sörensen, Baffi and Argentin. It was inspiring to see the front group still racing earnestly, although secure now from being caught. I moved in close as Sörensen stretched the leaders out on the long rise of the Capo Mele, his acceleration causing about 15 riders to drop off the pace at the back. Through the tunnel at the summit, and other attacks came from Del Tongo riders, then from Bugno's team; a war of nerves was being played out now, with each team determined to show the others they had a lot more still

to give, despite the tiredness that must surely be seeping though their legs. By the passage through Cervo, the teams had seemingly drawn a truce, preferring to save the racing until the last three climbs, the first of which – the Capo Berta – was almost upon them.

This year the Capo Berta was subdued thanks to the lack of team rivalries, and I took just a few obligatory shots as the three main teams kept things tightly together, more wary than ever now of using their dying reserves of energy. All that was left now was the long stretch of road leading to the Cipressa and, 15 kilometres later, the ramp of the Poggio.

Somewhere along this road two riders moved away; they'd gone on the descent of the Capo Berta immediately after a surge in the pace had been nullified over the summit. Angelo Canzonieri of Gis-Benotto, and Gianni Bugno of Chateau d'Ax, made a fine image as they pulled away on the road after the busy town of

. . . and cost me a finish picture of winner Gianni Bugno

Imperia, with its impressive hill-top castle overlooking the two fugitives' escape. I struggled to get both the two attackers and the spectacular background into my viewfinder, reasoning all the while that they would soon be caught. Their attack had brought the race to life, and from behind came the news that Gölz had counter-attacked, causing the 50-odd leaders to fragment within ten kilometres of the base of the Cipressa. I preferred to stay ahead now, trying to focus my thoughts on the final hour of the race, and on the final two hills.

We began the Cipressa ahead of the group containing Gölz, swinging excitedly off the sea road at San Lorenzo al Mare to begin the deceptively hard ascent. I revelled in the rush of adrenalin pumping through me, glad to have finally lost all recollection of the pathetic exit by Kelly's heroes. On the Cipressa, Bugno had gone on alone, the radio telling us that the Italian had a lead of 30 seconds over Gölz's group of perhaps 30 riders. And then the attacks came: first went Delion, then Argentin, followed by Jean-Claude Colotti. I moved in as much as possible, grabbing shots of these surges between the numerous hairpin bends of this six-kilometre climb. About two kilometres from the summit we moved ahead to Bugno, filming him from the right-hand side as the television motorbike of RAI hovered opposite us. Then, just after a sharp, rising right-hand bend, we pulled onto the grass verge, waiting with great anticipation for the next attacks behind Bugno.

The road rises straight ahead from the bend, and as the chasers swung into view I had a perfect view; Argentin had attacked, causing a further split in the chasers' ranks. I moved in close again, filming first Argentin's acceleration, then a counter-attack by Histor's Brian Holm, before dropping behind these two to seek the reaction. I got my best image of the race now – Fondriest bursting away from his rivals in pursuit of Argentin – and Bugno. I could see Colotti in my telephoto's sights, fighting to hang on to the Italian's pace with both men's open-mouthed expressions so strangely reinforced by their shaded glasses. We had to leave the race just before the summit, knowing the dangerous descent was no place to be caught amidst this attack; 1988 had given me images of a momentous crash on the Cipressa's descent, when an official's motorbike had caused a pile-up.

This time, instead of following the four riders that had spectacularly crashed in front of us that year, we shot down the descent behind Bugno. The blank-faced Italian wiggled through the village with its castle atop the Cipressa, and began his plunge downwards to the sea reaching the sanctuary of the sea road again, but with his lead reduced to just 20 seconds. Sensing Bugno was in with a chance, I got alongside him and fired off a series of shots before Torriani's car dropped in behind the race leader.

His presence cooled my ambitions for a moment, until I noticed that the old man seemed happy to let us work around Bugno; for once he wasn't shouting at us, Bugno being Italian. All the photographers massed alongside now, bringing a note of distinction to Bugno's attack; but I didn't think he could win – not this hitherto unsuccessful pro. My verdict lay in the group behind. We dropped back again, hearing the news that six chasers had grouped together on the descent: Gölz, Fondriest, Delion, Jesper Skibby, Colotti and Argentin. It had to be Argentin – or so I thought. Just five kilometres now separated Bugno, his six chasers and their mighty entourage from the start of the Poggio climb – the crux of the whole race. Sensing a great battle up there, I moved ahead and waited at the first viewpoint 500 metres up the climb.

All the memories of my previous adventures on this little climb came to mind – all the times when I'd 'bottled out', or miscalculated my timing on the Poggio; and then the time in 1989 when Fignon had made our jobs easier by attacking before the hill with Frans Maassen. Today's situation was not very different from last year's, with Bugno replacing Fignon as the joker in the pack by arriving on the hill alone. The Italian had left the sea road now, thrusting his tiring body onto the three-kilometre ascent. Patrice skilfully pulled ahead of Bugno as he approached us, but I took just a few shots here, wanting to preserve my nervous energy until we were nearer the top. As Bugno rode steadily into my sights, my open left eye could see the chasers barely 150 metres behind, pulling inexorably closer.

We dropped back again, instantly losing the attention of Torriani, who was obliged to stay ahead of Bugno. This wasn't a 'classic' Poggio battle; the numerical size of the contenders saw to that. Yet all the same my nerves tingled at the excitement of seeing the game played out before my very eyes. I was no longer nervous of the Poggio's reputation – no longer intimidated by the officials' shouts and threats; I was going to push my luck all the way today, filled with the experience borne of nearly ten years photographing this race.

Patrice placed me perfectly ahead of the six chasers, just long enough to record their collective ambitions; it wouldn't be long now. We accelerated away again, no doubt fooling the officials that we'd finished for the day, but merely biding our time. Just a few motorbikes remained near the race now: ourselves, Jacques Garcia's bike of *L'Equipe*, and Dutchman Cor Vos.

I dared another shot of Bugno and took a stationary shot on a left-hand bend. Once we'd stopped, the officials could do nothing but drive right past us now, their responsibility to oversee Bugno's attack being of greater priority. Free of intimidation, we hovered along the false flat in a no-man's-land, listening intently to the radio for news of the chase behind. I watched as Cor Vos accelerated away, his dire need of a finish picture forcing him to break free from the final battle.

Unheralded by our radio, a lone figure rode into view, through the shadows of the trees it took a few seconds to recognise Rolf Gölz; surely he was heading for victory, for barely a few seconds had passed since we'd let Bugno go. Patrice placed me perfectly as Gölz steamed into my sights, just a few metres behind our bike; I was really pushing my luck now. Patrice accelerated harshly away, filled with my instructions to

Eric Vanderaerden led the bunch home in 1991

pull in behind Gölz. As the adrenalin flowed, my experience told me that Gölz would catch Bugno on the descent, so we slowed up at the wide corner from where the real descent begins, and waited for Gölz's arrival there. We were alone now, the only photographer's bike left so close to the battle. I'd watched Garcia disappear down the descent right on the tail of Bugno's rear wheel, and cast aside any doubt that I'd made the right decision; Gölz came into view just half-a-dozen seconds later.

Patrice eased his bike out into the road in preparation, but just then a roadside *carabiniero* rushed out from the crowd and grabbed my jacket, determined to stop us following Gölz. I shrugged off his initial grip, yelling at Patrice to get us away; the young guard seemed determined to spoil our final play.

The policeman grabbed again, getting a stronger grip on my left arm this time, but fortunately Gölz was passing now and we accelerated cleanly away; the guardian's grip was torn loose, thankfully without my left arm. Relishing our exclusivity, I shot off a series of pictures as Gölz plunged on down.

Halfway down, the descent zigzags through a terraced plateau above the sea, dropping sinuously lower, while offering us a clear view of the road below; Bugno was well into Gölz's sights! I looked down onto the Italian's figure in time to see him looking up at Gölz, noticing also that the small cavalcade that had followed Bugno had now been pushed in front by officials. Yes, even they thought Bugno was finished. We continued on down – just Gölz, ourselves and a solitary radio informer poised for Gölz's greatest moment – although he had still to outsprint Bugno.

There was just 50 metres in it now – but then it all began to go wrong. So fired up was I that I hadn't noticed how close the end of the descent was. Only as we passed below the small red flag indicating the last kilometre in the race, did I realise that Gölz had not made any further gain, and that his capture of Bugno was not so certain after all. Since 1988 the finish of the Milan–San Remo has been brought back towards the foot of the hill by more than a kilometre, relieving the busy town, famous for its jazz, of some serious congestion on a Saturday afternoon. What it's meant for both photographers and cyclists is that only 800 metres now separate the finish line from their last contact with the Poggio – good today for Bugno, bad for Rolf Gölz and myself.

Now in the long finishing straight my error became clear, Patrice accelerated past Gölz, reading my thoughts in a last-ditch effort to get to the finish ahead of Bugno, who was stretched out over his bars on the run-in to the finish. Five-hundred metres were left: we tried to go to the left of Bugno, only to be foiled by a motorbike official; 80 metres further, and Patrice now switched to the right, but again a motorcycle official barred our way. Faced with this human barrier, as well as the implications if we barged through so close to the line, I pulled Patrice back and conceded defeat: in less than one kilometre, my anticipated scoop had turned into disaster; I was going to miss the finish.

Bugno rode towards the line – towards the massed ranks of photographers crouched on both sides of the road. It must certainly have been a great image, with Bugno jubilantly waving his arms high in the air as he drew closer to his greatest victory. I'm sure the convoy following him was equally impressive, as it always is when Milan–San Remo winners ride into town – television cameras, sponsors' vehicles, officials' motorbikes and the organiser's car. The finishing shots of Bugno must have had it all – the moment an Italian had won the *Primavera* for all of Italy. I found no solace in the shots I'd taken from behind as Bugno reached the line, nor in the pictures that appeared around Europe in the weeks that followed – for there, in amongst the finish shots, were Patrice and I, embarrassingly caught in our worst moment for all to see.

I made the quickest possible exit from San Remo that afternoon, avoiding any confrontation that might be awaiting me should I encounter an official. Torriani had seemed particularly angry, but then we had crossed the finish line as unwelcome guests alongside his car. Such had been the excitement of the last hour that I'd almost completely forgotten the disappointment of the day, when the favourites had got left behind. Their ignominious departure from the race seemed so distant now. Patrice was speeding me at 140 kilometres per hour towards Nice for a 7-pm flight to London. I couldn't get home quickly enough – it had been quite a day.

SEAN KELLY

21 MARCH 1992: MILAN–SAN REMO

We were racing towards the Poggio – the photographers and 40 or more victory-hungry cyclists battling along the sea road of the Italian Riviera, heading for an encounter with the famous hill above San Remo. Behind us were the warriors of the 83rd Milan–San Remo, and amongst them the oldest warrior of them all – Sean Kelly. In there too was Moreno Argentin, the red-hot favourite in a race that has never been kind to its favourites, as well as men such as Maurizio Fondriest and Rolf Sörensen. Never before had public conviction been so strong in declaring that one man would succeed where others would fail – but could Argentin win? Six of his Ariostea team-mates thought so: they were driving the big group that had formed after the Cipressa, and were hurtling at a demonic pace towards their encounter with on the Poggio, just ten kilometres away now.

A 'Z'-team rider attacked at the foot of the climb, the figure raced into my sights, it was Frenchman Eric Boyer, I fired off a few frames before moving away. Behind him the orange-and-yellow jerseys of Ariostea were chasing hard, the identities of their wearers hard to distinguish in the fading light. Boyer's effort ended just one kilometre after it had begun, to be replaced by a sudden jump from Argentin himself.

Patrice got me right alongside the flying Italian just long enough to grab a few precious shots in the face of severe pressure from the Italian TV motorbike and race officials: what a battle! I was pained to see that Argentin's attack had been hindered by some of the very motorbikes that surrounded him, but grew excited when Argentin accelerated again; this was unprecedented action. We got in close, banging right against the TV motorbike, whose driver was doggedly holding onto his territory. Once again the aggressor's attack came to nothing as Fondriest pulled his compatriot back. Just five kilometres remained, and the real hill had ended, to be replaced by the illusory false flat that had always proved so decisive in the Milan–San Remo.

Only three photographers remained close to the action: myself, Cor Vos and *L'Equipe's* cameraman that had dared to stay this late. Patrice took me back one last time, and Argentin successfully attacked at that very instant a few metres behind us. I banged off all the frames I could in the few seconds I had, and shouted to Patrice to get away before the real descent began; Argentin was away and racing manicly.

As we sped down the sinuous road, I looked back anxiously at the figures descending a few *lacets* above us. Just a few seconds after I had glimpsed the lone figure of Argentin and the accompanying press motorbikes, the chasers sped into view, preceded by an unidentifiable lone chaser, who couldn't have been more than 50 metres behind!

We sped up to the finishing line, but I'd barely taken my place in the photographers' ranks before the announcer shouted to an astonished audience: 'Kelly *con* Argentin! Kelly *con* Argentin!' I was staggered: Sean Kelly, at nearly 36 years of age, had caught Argentin on the descent of the Poggio – a feat unprecedented in any Milan–San Remo I'd known. It all seemed unreal, impossible. Barely half a minute later, two figures raced into view around the angled finishing straight. It was Kelly – Kelly by a mile, a yard, an inch? Who cared anyway? Sean Kelly won the Milan–San Remo in the most incredible way. The battle of the Poggio had never been more keenly contested.

The scene at St Niklaas in 1990

TOUR OF FLANDERS

Land of forests, of canals; land of windmills, of hills; land of poplar trees, of war; land of peace – Belgium is also the land of cycle racing, home to legendary men such as Rik Van Steenbergen and Rik Van Looy, Roger De Vlaeminck and Eddy Merckx, Claude Criquielion and the Planckaert dynasty. Belgium is the land of the spring classics, of races like the Tour of Flanders, Ghent–Wevelgem, Flèche Wallonne and Liège–Bastogne–Liège. Belgium is a wonderful place to be in spring-time.

Imagine a country so perfect for cycle racing: the forested hills and valleys of the south, through which the courses follow meandering highways over the rise and fall of the terrain, and where sheer narrow ascents lie hidden in the landscape; and the contrast of the north, as different from the south as the language of its people, where the highways are exchanged for winding lanes and farm tracks, and where misshapen, cobblestoned ascents provide another form of sport altogether. Whether in Wallonie or in Flanders, cycle racing has a unique place in the hearts of the Belgian nation – a place filled with memories so rich and deep that few people could seriously question Belgium's claim to be the centre of the cycling world.

1 APRIL 1990: ST NIKLAAS

The mahogany-lined walls of Committee Room One, set deep inside the grandiose surroundings of St Niklaas' town hall, seem at once threatening and inspiring – a result perhaps of the sense of history that permeates such façades. Built in 1878, the hugely ornate town hall has survived throughout Belgium's territorial ravages, so that its massive edifice means far more to the people of St Niklaas than merely a building that dominates the town. It seems a fitting place to host such a grand occasion as the start of the Tour of Flanders.

On a warm, sunny Sunday in April, a different sense of occasion is experienced by the assortment of men crowded into the antechamber. It is the voice of Albert Florquen, a *kommandant* in the Flanders police, that makes the biggest impression as the minutes tick by to the start of Belgium's greatest classic. Florquen is a veteran of nine Tours of Flanders. He policed his first 'Ronde' in 1984, at a time when only half-a-dozen motorcycle photographers followed the races in Belgium, and has become a great fan of cycle racing in the process. His task today is a familiar one – to ensure the safe and correct conduct of all the vehicles in the race, most especially the mobile photographers, whose numbers are now resolutely set at 13, having four years earlier jumped to an unruly 22.

The words of the *kommandant* boom across the vast room with all the assertion that one expects from such a high ranking official. 'Respect and obey the instructions of my men, and I can promise you a rewarding day here in Flanders', the rotund police chief exclaims, a slight upward curl of his lips betraying how much he relishes the occasion. 'Disrespect will not be tolerated – you have the choice, and you know the consequences.' The man had chosen his words carefully, and had delivered them with a slow certainty lest anyone should doubt his sincerity. Yet few amongst us doubted him for a moment, nor the gravity of the day's work ahead of us; the Ronde van Vlaanderen, to give the race its full Flemish title, is without doubt the most difficult of all the great races to photograph.

The race's natural obstacles are intimidating enough – 13 sinuously woven 'bergs', whose placement just into the second half of the race seems to conspire totally against our freedom to work as the race reaches its ferocious crescendo amongst the so-called Flemish Ardennes – but it's the pressure that emanates from within the determined peloton that incites the most trepidation amongst race followers. A Tour of Flanders peloton is like no other, for it has an almost undying will to survive, together, regardless of what man and nature can throw against it.

No amount of pressure will ever break that human

Jelle Nijdam didn't make it as far as the Oude Kwaremont in 1988

cord of unity – a factor that makes it a nightmare for the likes of us photographers, who need to move around the peloton during the day. The roads can rise, fall, twist and turn, snake through towns and villages along the way; the riders can be threatened by rain-slicked surfaces and blasted by the strongest winds; they may even be delayed by a closed railway crossing: but nothing will induce the group to fragment – not, that is, until Wannegem-Lede, where the first cobbles lie in waiting, and where the first of the day's climbs, the Oude Kwaremont, looms on the horizon. It's at Wannegem-Lede that the very living soul of this peloton is finally endangered, its hitherto unshakable spirit shattered by a sudden descending turn out of the village onto a seven-foot-wide farm track. From then on the day is a series of pursuits and captures and pursuits once again, as the tenacious body of men struggles desperately against the inevitable verdict of the 13 climbs.

Although the threat of those first cobbles at Wannegem-Lede is still some three hours, or 130

kilometres distant, from the start at St Niklaas, their strategic influence on the race weighs heavily on my mind as I move down the majestic stone stairway into the massive square with the words of the *kommandant* still ringing in my ears. Outside, with 20 minutes to go, the Tour of Flanders could not have found a more perfect setting for the race start. The burghers of St Niklaas are proud of their claim to have the biggest town square in the whole of Belgium. And when, in 1977, the townspeople had lured the race start from the grasp of their regional rivals in Ghent, it seemed the ideal way to put St Niklaas on the world map. Later police estimates would put the size of the crowd today at around 10,000, each and every one of them race enthusiasts to the core. On any other day of the year, the square would naturally be dominated by the 180-foot-high steeple that towers above the roof of the town hall – on any other day!

Today, every eye is focused on a massive catwalk directly in front of the town hall. Erected across the full width of the square, this eight-foot-high platform is

The windmill near Wannegem–Lede in 1989, where 7-Eleven's Roy Knickman leads the way

where all of the 198 starters are required to 'sign on', riding their bicycles across the apparatus in full view of the milling crowd to register for the race. This show-business-style presentation was initiated by the Tour of Flanders' organisers in 1988, as a way to celebrate the race's 70th anniversary. Its establishment replaced the chaotic procedure of having everyone – riders, press, officials and police – carry out their pre-race scramble inside the town hall. So popular was the new concept that people travelled in from miles around, drawn to St Niklaas by the chance of a free show, many of them still dressed in their Sunday suits from an early-morning visit to church.

We photographers scuttle away for a last-minute glance at race maps and to debate the day's plans with their drivers. Our race radios have to be checked – an annoyingly slow procedure that only adds to the anxiety on such an important occasion. As usual, it's the foreigners such as myself whose radio is checked last – an act I interpret as a warning to behave from the Belgian race officials. The police briefing was aimed especially at those foreign drivers and photographers who might be thinking they are exempt from Belgium's highway laws.

With all our credentials finally secured, there remain but a few minutes in which to do what we're actually paid to do. There's even barely time to snap a headshot of Vanderaerden or Fignon before the commissaire's whistle blows and the starter's ceremonial gun fires, signalling a chaotic rush for our drivers in order to follow the peloton out of the square before the crowds block our path. With a pair of helicopters clattering overhead, with two-dozen police sirens wailing in our ears, and with whistle-blowing officials already starting their day-long panic and confusion, the Tour of Flanders race entourage finally quits St Niklaas, deliberately conducting a full circuit of the square to prolong its rather pompous send-off.

It's at this moment, for the first time in 48 hours, that I can at last relax, happy to be away from the crowded

The incident in 1987 that led to the Koppenberg's closure; Denmark's Jesper Skibby loses his balance at the steepest point . . .

... the BWB car approaches and drives over Skibby's bike, almost crushing his feet ...
... a fan rushes to the rescue

square, happy too to be on the road and free to do my work. Each year, as we move away from St Niklaas, I recall the nightmare of 1982, when I was anything but relaxed: I'd arrived at St Niklaas just as the race was leaving! That year, I'd failed to notice that continental Europe had moved one hour ahead of Britain during the night – an oversight that necessitated frantic pleading with race officials before I was allowed to join the race, taking my credentials on the move from the organiser's car. It's an oversight that still brings the inevitable tease from my continental colleagues – a reaction not helped by my having repeated the mistake in a French race in 1990!

It's out on the road to Eeklo, with the breeze in our faces, and with the welcome sunshine lighting on the kaleidoscope of colours formed by the riders' backs, that life in the wake of the Flanders peloton can be finely savoured. It's a time for brief greetings between the photographers – those that didn't travel south in mid-March for the Milan–San Remo classic – and for a somewhat cooler acknowledgement of the Belgian officials travelling alongside and behind us in their cars.

The relationship between photographers and officials in Belgium is unique, fragile, and one ever likely to fragment in such a race as the Tour of Flanders. Just as the devil-may-care attitude of the Italian race is replaced by an intimidated restraint in Belgium, so too is the comparative warmth of Italy's officials soon forgotten in the face of the oppressive rules laid down by the gentlemen from the nation's cycling governing body, the Belgisch Wielrijdersbond (BWB).

It is officials from that body who seek most vehemently to control our movements during the race – determined, it often seems, by some unclear motive to make our job as difficult as possible. The position of their car – directly behind the simmering peloton, and to our right – enables them to administer their task with apparent ease. The BWB's task is a very necessary one, given the restrictions enforced on the race by the narrowness of many of the roads, by the peculiarity of the race pattern, and by the requirements of the nation's television company, BRT. Yet the undisguised pleasure its officials take in their role, and the manner in which they carry it out, will never endear them to any of our profession.

It's from the BWB officials' car, a silver-grey BMW, that the classics in Belgium are controlled, its four occupants responsible for a variety of roles within the race. This involves either using the car's VHF transmitter to make contact or, more usually, barking orders at us from an open window. We also know that the services of *Kommandant* Florquen can be called upon to drive a point home.

The adrenalin build-up to the Tour of Flanders will have begun many days earlier for me, whilst still in England. A sense of anticipation, coupled with a strong hint of trepidation, serves to heighten my awareness of the occasion – a state of mind accentuated earlier that same morning by the realisation that it has been a full three weeks since the Milan–San Remo provided a nerve-jangling introduction to the season of the one-day classics.

Photographing a one-day race has an attraction all of its own – one very different from a three-week-long stage race, where an air of calm hovers over each day's racing. In a one-day classic – and especially the Tour of Flanders – there's no such thing as tomorrow. And with this fact comes an innate subconscious tension that affects everyone in the race, making life hard for those of us that follow in the breezy wake of the peloton, but nevertheless guaranteeing us an adventurous day out.

The routing of the Tour of Flanders is basically the same each year, moving in an approximately westerly direction away from the Antwerp region towards Bruges, skirting north of its former start host, Ghent, to form the beginnings of a rectangular course that is devised to live up to the name of the race. A long southern thrust then takes the race into the hotbed cycling area around Kortrijk, from where the route turns eastwards, carrying the by now madly accelerating cyclists towards

A more usual scene on the Koppenberg

the Flemish Ardennes around Oudenaarde. One hour and ten 'bergs' later, the race resumes its eastward course in the direction of Brussels, playing its finale between the brutal ascent on the Wall of Geraardsbergen (Grammont) and the final climb of the race, the Bosberg. Just twelve kilometres separate the crest of the Bosberg and the popular finish in Meerbeke – a village on the outskirts of the market town of Ninove that first received the finish of 'De Ronde' in 1973.

This rectangular-shaped course has hardly changed since the first Tour of Flanders in 1913, when just 37 men started. The Tour has always started in the north, has always had Kortrijk as its halfway mark, and in postwar years its finale has always been fought out in the hills of southern Flanders. Only here are there to be found significant changes to the route, the most

publicised being the introduction, and (eleven years later) the exclusion, of the Koppenberg. If there has been one identifying mark about the Tour of Flanders, it is the Koppenberg. Quickly gaining attention for the absurdity of its inclusion in the 1976 route, this 600-metre-long cobbled monster established its real *legende* the following year, when the Belgian cyclist Freddy Maertens took an illegal bike change from his brother on the hill. Maertens then began what would have been a race-winning breakaway with Roger De Vlaeminck, had he not been told of his disqualification on the road to Meerbeke. Consequently the reigning world champion withdrew his challenge to De Vlaeminck in the sprint.

Every year, one incident or another brought notoriety to the Koppenberg, and if there was insufficient drama

The Koppenberg, 1985: Paul Sherwen takes a Sunday-afternoon stroll with Laurent Fignon . . .

to be had from such an incident, then the sheer spectacle of seeing more than 200 professionals scrambling afoot up the 22-percent gradient more than assured the hill's notoriety for another year. By 1987 the Koppenberg had already outlived its authenticity in a sport becoming more sophisticated by the moment, and when the Danish rider Jesper Skibby had the misfortune to fall on the cobbles and almost have his feet crushed by an official car, the Koppenberg sadly but dramatically disappeared from the next year's itinerary.

The incident with Skibby has an amusing relevance to those of us that still photograph 'De Ronde', for that day we photographed the very same BWB car that so nearly crushed Skibby's left foot! It's therefore hardly surprising that the officials seem to dislike us so much, as pictures of the incident were blazoned across the front pages of newspapers in Belgium, Holland and France the next morning, exposing the BWB's unsporting behaviour to a critical public. On the Wednesday following that year's Tour of Flanders, the BWB took revenge on us in the Ghent–Wevelgem, employing the Belgian police to make our lives harder than usual in the closing stages. Things have never been the same since.

Kwaremont, Patersberg, Taaienberg, Eikenberg – the names roll familiarly around in my mind now, 30 minutes down the road from St Niklaas, still two-and-a-half hours before those cobbles at Wannegem-Lede. The first half-hour since leaving St Niklaas has given welcome respite after the bustling pomposity of the start there, and I've done nothing more than simply speed along behind the racing group, slowly collecting

Allan Peiper takes the Patersberg in his stride in 1990

my thoughts for the day ahead. I make a point of sharing these thoughts with my driver too, so that once the serious work begins he is completely aware of my mood, and with it the manner in which we will tackle the race. My *motard* today is Patrice, a trusty captain if ever there was one, though I know he is nervous in this, his first drive in a Belgian race.

Until 1989 it was always possible that a small domestic team would use these early kilometres to gain publicity by sending one of its riders up the road in an apparently suicidal breakaway. But with the formation of the World Cup, and the accompanying restrictions on which teams could even race in a classic such as the Tour of Flanders, the likeliness of such surprises has all but disappeared as far as this tactic-dominated race is concerned.

Over the years, dozens of incidents have justified the importance of seeing a race the whole way through; and in Flanders, at least, there is always that wonderful countryside to compensate in those occasional years when nothing of note has occurred. I'd also developed a desire, almost a greed, to see the race the whole way through lest I should miss something special. After about 30–40 kilometres I bid my colleagues a temporary goodbye, leaving them to succumb to the gourmet delights of some inviting Oudenaarde restaurant, convincing myself that today something is going to happen, though all the while envying their freedom of mind that enables them to turn their backs on this great race before it has almost started. Alas, by the time we arrive 30 kilometres from that very spot, I know that they, and not me, have made the right decision.

The fast start only lasted a dozen more kilometres from the turn-off point, and the ensuing procession across Bruges and then south to Kortrijk has only contained a smattering of incidents, but not one crash, nor even a hint of one. There was, however, a difficult moment when we tried to overtake the peloton around Deerlijk in order to get ahead of the pack before those first cobbles, but nothing more exciting than that. We had misjudged the right moment to pass them, as what had initially been a wide highway suddenly became a twisty passage through a small village. To make matters worse, the riders chose that moment to begin their sudden acceleration for the hills up ahead, and there we were, stuck a quarter of the way down the peloton, completely locked into the seething mass, with cyclists fore and aft, and with a six-inch-high kerbstone to seal our discomfort.

It's at times like this that I'd rather be elsewhere, and that's exactly what the riders wished upon us, telling us so in no uncertain terms and in at least three languages. It is extremely stressful being carried amidst such a hive of energy and tension, where a little mistake by one cyclist or one motorcyclist could spell disaster. Looking over Patrice's shoulder, I see a cyclist inches in front of us, battling desperately to sneak through to a better position ahead. I tense every time his shoulders rub one of his colleagues, and cringe when someone further up front applies his brakes, sending a ripple of panic through the section of the peloton behind him. Even worse is the knowledge that a line of cyclists is pacing precariously in our slipstream; heaven help all of us if there's a crash! But Patrice keeps his nerve amongst the cursing and swearing, not remotely troubled when one particular cyclist leans on our left-hand wing mirror to steady himself after a sudden swerve in the centre of the pack. Slowly but surely, he inches his way through the jostling mélée to reach haven as the road suddenly clears ahead. I suspect he actually revels in situations like this.

The cobbles at Wannegem-Lede provide me with a major decision: to go in front or behind? I elected to get well-ahead, wanting to try a shot of the race passing beside a massive windmill that towers over the cobbled course. I know it's important to emerge off the cobbles at the head of the race, for not to do so will affect my mobility around the race for some time to come, the narrow tracks following this one will afford no possibility of passing. But a windmill is a windmill, and for me an exciting element in any picture of a bike race in Flanders or Holland.

Everything is perfect: blue skies, perfect lighting, little wind – an unusual mix for a Tour of Flanders but nevertheless an ideal one for photography. A full 15 minutes have elapsed before the sound of the approaching helicopter raises picnicking spectators from their chosen places: the race is about to arrive. I take yet another light reading, focus again on the spot where I expect to release my first frame, and glance nervously at the approaching dust clouds that I know contain the Tour of Flanders peloton. Our race radio crackles into life informing us in Flemish, then French, that the riders are on the first cobblestones. 'Any moment now', I think. Then it happens. Just as the riders begin to emerge into my sights, the radio coughs again, bringing with it the news I least want to hear: 'Valpartij, Sean Kelly.'

Valpartij was the second Flemish word I ever learned, the first one being of course unprintable. In no uncertain terms it means crash – literally 'fall-party' – which is why, in the land of cycle racing, I learned of its meaning so soon. But it's the words 'Sean Kelly' that have jolted my thoughts. What was he doing, falling so early in the race, in fact falling at all? But I have little time to continue that line of thought as the race sweeps into view, forcing me to forget any notion I might have of sprinting back down the road to where I assume Kelly lies.

Within 20 seconds half the peloton has passed me by, and I seize the opportunity to jump back on the bike behind Patrice in the hope that we may get onto the course before the rest of the field come along, bringing with them the following team cars that will hinder our

chances of repassing the race. Not surprisingly we fail: Kelly's fall may have split the field in two, but the stragglers were determined to catch up at this still early stage, and we were too slow to move out before they came by. That's always the price to pay in the Tour of Flanders, where a fine balance exists between getting a good shot and ruining your whole day in the process.

Eventually Patrice sped off behind the team cars, immediately profiting from placing his bike on the slim shoulder of dirt at the side of the track. We inched our way past the team cars one by one, barely able to see more than a few feet in front, such was the level of dust being thrown up. At times like this I never know whether to look and risk getting a eyeful of dust, or hide myself behind the driver's shoulders. I chose the latter, but kept my eyes half open anyway as Patrice worked his way up the convoy, occasionally flicking his bike further off the track as a car's sudden movement ahead indicated trouble. I tried not to take in the close proximity of a deep rain ditch a few inches to our right. I also tried not to notice the closeness of the Ariostea car directly in front as it swung viciously into our path in an attempt to reach one of its riders. Surely Patrice wouldn't be able to stop in time if he had to. Thankfully, he'd already seen the car driver's target, and slipped left into a too small gap in order to get around the trouble. Out of the corner of my squinting dust-filled eye, I glimpsed Rolf Sörensen at the side of the road, holding his back wheel in the air as the service car drew up.

This cobbled conveyor belt finally ended more than three kilometres after it had first begun, and its destruction had a spectacular effect on the race. Rider after rider had fallen victim to one thing or another here – a puncture, a crash, a close encounter with a rival's team car, or even a brush with a marauding spectator. But the outcome was all the same for those left stranded: instant banishment from the remainder of the day's racing. Fortunately Patrice's 1000cc BMW engine helped us escape from such trouble, and by the time we felt tarmac beneath our wheels again, his skill had put us ahead of the leading team car.

Now we were in a series of narrow twisting lanes, and I realised how smashed-up the peloton was. Standing up on the motorbike, I could see the damage. Ahead of us were five separated sections of what had once been virtually a single living body, each section now containing anything between 10 and 30 cyclists hell-bent on getting back into the race before the next stretch of cobbles hit them.

Behind us it was a different story, and looking back through the line of team cars I spotted individuals riding for all they were worth to get across to the front of the race, darting manically in and out between the team cars if they were lucky to have this protection, or simply plugging away in the no-man's-land that lay behind the cars. But none of these groups contained our hero Kelly; on reaching smooth terrain, the official speaker had announced that Kelly had dropped out due to a suspected broken collar-bone. I cursed to myself, wishing I hadn't chosen to get ahead for those first cobbles. For I knew I'd have caught Kelly's crash if I'd placed myself behind the peloton. Even the most poignant shot of a Flemish windmill couldn't make up for a dramatic one of Sean Kelly lying broken in a ditch.

Kelly or no Kelly, the Tour of Flanders was waiting for no one today, and the snaking line maintained its speed on its meander through Flemish farmlands lit so attractively by the bright sunshine. But we could go nowhere with the race still split to ribbons. Ten frustrating minutes passed, with no chance to get ahead, before the village of Kerkhove appeared on the horizon, and with it a wide enough road to speed by just as the feeding station loomed.

We headed straight for the Oude Kwaremont, still more than ten kilometres away, for there was more to be gained by getting a good vantage point there than by hanging back with the main group that was now enjoying a short lull after the first sortie onto the *pavé*. Surprisingly, nearly all the little groups had joined up again – a legacy of the fine weather conditions, I mused.

The Oude Kwaremont starts out of the back of the town of Kluisbergen, utilising a tiny lane to squeeze and then squirt the riders onto a rising gradient that steepens at the exact point where the tarmacadam surface turns uncaringly into cobbles. Like many of the 'bergs' in today's race, the Oude Kwaremont has lost a lot of its cobbled longevity in the cause of better roads. But a preservation order now exists to safeguard these sacred climbs from further depletion. It's because of this that the cobbles of the Kwaremont only begin halfway up. There are two choices here for the photographer: either he picks a spot on the steeper, crowd-packed section of the climb, just before it passes through the village centre of Kwaremont; or he does what I usually do, which is to go on ahead to the second, flatter section, where the real damage caused by the steep section can be both photographed and assessed.

Time here is of the essence, no matter which option is chosen; for the Patersberg is just five kilometres away along the race route, and is simply to good to miss! I recalled an item in the morning's meeting stating that any motorbikes approaching the Patersberg less than ten minutes before the race would be diverted away. Rules, rules, rules!

Feeling lucky despite missing Kelly's crash, I pulled Patrice up just a few hundred metres before the end of the cobbles, and began a short but anxious wait for a sighting of the race. Despite the speed with which we'd left the race behind at Kerkhove, the peloton was already in the village of Kluisbergen: my radio told me that. So it also told the dozens of spectators now milling around the bike, curious to know what had happened in the race so far. They dispersed as the helicopter approached, leaving me to gather my crumbling thoughts on what to do here.

From where I stood, I had a clear view of the pretty church steeple that marked the centre of Kwaremont, and therefore a clear view of the snaking line of cyclists that was threading its way onto this set of cobbles. A red jersey was leading the race – my 300mm lens told

In the wet conditions of 1989, the Taaienberg was a cyclist's nightmare and a photographer's delight

me that – and 30 seconds later the easily recognisable figure of Eddy Planckaert rode into view, tracked closely by Claude Criquielion and Adrie Van der Poel.

With my work done we were soon accelerating off into the tail-enders, waiting for our chance at the end of the cobbles to get by on the big main road to Ronse. At the end of the track, the cyclists cross over the main road and into Ronde van Vlaanderenstraat, so named in recognition of the first time the Oude Kwaremont was included in the race in 1919. We, however, turned sharp left onto the Ronse highway, and sped flat-out to a small lane on the left, with the intention of arriving there a few precious minutes before the race came in from the right – still on its original route – to go down the same lane.

The lanes leading to the Patersberg are perilous indeed, sometimes just five feet wide, and dropping ever more steeply into the valley. It was in these lanes in 1982 that my driver had gone too fast into one of the many hidden curves and, unable to stop, had carried straight on into a ploughed field. That had been the first time I'd been allowed into the race on a motorbike, and the ensuing delay as we dragged the heavy bike out of the mud meant I'd completely missed the Koppenberg. Today I had a more skilful driver, and Patrice steered us confidently amongst the picturesque hills that I knew contained the Patersberg, where the crazy stuff really begins. All the time the race radio kept crackling into life, informing us of one incident or another in the race behind us, while at the same time serving as a reminder that they weren't very far behind. I warned Patrice not to stop on any account at the junction with the hill, lest an over-anxious steward should try to stop us going onto the climb; we were desperately late.

A steward made a half-hearted attempt to stop us, but Patrice put paid to that one's chance of glory by driving straight at him, forcing the poor man to concede. The Patersberg, lined five deep with short-sleeved

47

Eric Vanderaerden heads for victory in 1985

spectators, made for an impressive sight as we drove up the 500-metre hill to the top, where I left Patrice with the other drivers and ran back down amongst the madness. It's hard to stand up there on such a landmark and not be moved by the Flemings' great passion for cycling. All down the hill, a mass of people buzzed eagerly at the excitement of the day, their colourful throng cutting an impressive path down the lush green hillside. No doubt just as many people would still have been there even if it had been pouring with rain.

As I took my spot on the hill, squatting close against the metal barriers so as not to spoil the spectators' view, I reminded myself of the amusing history of the Patersberg, which has almost gone forgotten in the wake of the Koppenberg's demise. In 1984, a local farmer, jealous of a neighbour whose house lay right at the side of the Koppenberg, decided to create his own cobbled climb, declaring in national newspapers his dream of

seeing the Tour of Flanders pass over *his* hill. The idea had the blessing of *Het Nieuwsblad*, the newspaper that organised the race. For they believed a diversion onto the as yet unmade Patersberg was just the thing to prolong the Koppenberg's existence – that this new hill would sort out the riders and thus reduce the heavily criticised chaos on the Koppenberg. Within 18 months, and through his own personal efforts, the farmer had laid a cobbled path into what had until then been an innocuous-looking hillside, and in the early spring of 1986 the organisers announced the addition of this newest 'attraction' to the Tour of Flanders. As today's race approached the hill, I thought to myself that this could only have happened in Belgium.

From the upper slopes of the hill it was possible to see the first cyclists descending that very same narrow lane that we'd just driven along, their growing visibility in the hazy valley bringing the thousands on the hill to full voice. 'Van der Poel!' shouted one fan, determined to be the first within earshot to put a name to one of the tiny figures down below. Another fan answered with his own declaration – 'Planckaert!' – while another cried 'Vanderaerden!' Soon the air became full of some of the greatest names in competition, most of them of Dutch origin, with the exception of one brave man who was heard yelling for Fignon. As the mêlée of spectators below bobbed and weaved, and the television motorbike hove into view through the wall of emotion, the first men were seen fighting the hill, the gradient, the noise.

In fact it was Steve Bauer who came by first, closely marked by Jean-Marie Wampers and Guido Bontempi. Then came a swarm of familiar figures, each of them in his own awkward way carving a desperate path to the top just 100 metres ahead. Behind the first wave of 30 a different scene developed. The faces were still familiar, but these men were walking – very clumsily too in their cycling shoes. I'd barely had time to refocus before the figure of Moreno Argentin came into view, pedalling quickly through the carnage of men pushing bikes. Some of them looked up from their purgatory, startled by the ease with which the Italian was tackling the hill, and no doubt annoyed at how easily this Latin was making fools of the Belgians in their own land.

Patrice eagerly took off into the race, aware of my instructions to him about getting ahead before the Taaienberg. Even now, with just two cobbled hills gone, my mind was already in a daze, confused partly by the speed at which everything was happening, and partly by the growing anxiety that I wasn't getting the pictures I wanted.

However, there was still a long way to go – about 120 kilometres, in fact. I took comfort in those thoughts, but couldn't fail to recall previous Tours of Flanders, tours that had been wet and cold, but which had thrown up great photo opportunities, tours that would already have split the race asunder. There again, I was warm and dry.

Just ten kilometres separate the Patersberg and the Taaienberg. Some of the narrowest, snakiest lanes in Flanders have to be negotiated at this point – lanes that would be challenging enough in normal driving conditions, but never more so than with cyclists weaving all over the place, half-crazed in their determination to close the gap ahead to the next pocket of riders. It was like a mirror image of what had happened after the cobbles at Wannegem-Lede, but here the damage was deeper, and so obviously irredeemable for most of the men now chasing.

Patrice worked his way past cyclist after cyclist, some of them in groups of half a dozen, but mostly in twos or threes. Slowly but surely we drew closer to the leading group, whose presence on the serpentine road ahead was well highlighted by the TV helicopter and a small phalanx of cars and motorbikes. Occasionally Patrice was forced onto the grass by a sudden swerve from a cyclist. At one scary moment, he actually chose to overtake by using the uneven grass verge.

It's at times like this – when the pressure's on, when the race is stretched to splitting point, when you see the likes of Gianni Bugno, Jelle Nijdam and Dirk de Wolf

unable to keep pace – that the tough reality of their profession hits home. It is not like the Paris–Roubaix, where the cobbles gradually break a peloton into pieces; here in Flanders it is sheer physiological destruction. It is the power of the strong men on the cobbled climbs, and the speed of their accelerations between each hill, that impress most. And on this serpent road to the Taaienberg it is one of the most impressive things to be seen. In a 'normal' Tour of Flanders, the Taaienberg is perhaps the most crucial element in the race, coming at a point when most men have given their all and are simply unable to give any more.

Year after year, in the rush to catch up after the Patersberg, the photographers' motorbikes usually find themselves stuck behind the first big group as the Taaienberg looms up, having failed to negotiate their way past the shredded field in the intervening ten kilometres. The Taaienberg is steep – in places as steep as the Wall of Geraardsbergen. It's also very narrow, invariably covered in a green moss, and on a 'normal' day extremely slippery. There's a belief that teams deliberately instruct a rider to fall, knowing his obstruction of the others will help a team-mate's chances in front. Either way, it makes for chaos at the back, and with motorbikes following on the chaos is accentuated.

For photographers like myself, who wish to record an overall impression of the Tour of Flanders, this chaos is it. My favourite anecdote from the Taaienberg stems from the 1989 race – a 'normal' Tour of Flanders if ever there was one, with heavy rain that had been falling for hours even before we'd reached the hill. As in every year, we'd tried to get ahead of the leading group, and as in every year we'd failed, frustrated by the difficulties of the narrow roads and by the obstructiveness of race officials scared at letting us past.

We'd arrived at the foot of the Taaienberg directly behind a 50-man group – the largest surviving unit following a Van der Poel attack on the Patersberg. No sooner had our wheels touched the glistening surface of cobbles than a movement from within the group

Moreno Argentin leads Rudy Dhaenens on the Bosberg in 1990 . . .

ahead of us sparked off a series of calamitous events. Clearly someone had fallen over on the cobbles. Others had been forced to stop as they lost traction on the cobblestones. And then it was our turn – a dozen-strong group of leather-clad motorcyclists rammed right up behind the growing chaos, unwittingly about to become very much part of that chaos. As the riders ahead of us began to dismount *en masse*, unable as they were to continue by wheel, so our engines stalled in the sudden deceleration. Within seconds the hill was blocked by the walking cyclists, and most definitely blocked at the back by the stalled motorbikes. Sensing an unprecedented picture opportunity here, I scampered up the hill, struggling to keep my footing on the cobbles as I dodged between each fallen or walking cyclist. Within 50 metres of the last cobbles, I took sanctuary in the water-filled gutter that ran down each side of the six-foot-wide track and ran off as many pictures as I could before the rain obscured my camera's optics – and what images they were!

That memory might be one-year old, but its impression on me was so great that it could easily have taken place yesterday. However, at least I'd got to the hill first this time around. Not since 1979 had I been granted a view of the front of the race, when Francesco Moser had ridden so majestically at the head of affairs. And then I hadn't been on a motorbike. Today I took my place at the same spot as in 1989 and waited barely a minute before the first cyclists arrived, who were led this time by Maurizio Fondriest, looking unusually confident at this stage. Even more surprising were the figures determinedly following him: a Swiss, Rolf Jarmann, and a Dane, Per Pedersen. Then the figure of Eddy Planckaert brought an air of respectability to this acceleration, and when his Panasonic team-mate Allan Peiper heaved across my sights to join the break, I knew that at last, with 83 kilometres still to go, the race was well and truly on.

Quickly, things began to happen. Another Italian, Argentin, came into view, followed immediately by Laurent Fignon and the two Belgians Michel Dernies and Rudy Dhaenens. I ran into a small gap between the

... while behind, Maurizio Fondriest crosses the summit of the Bosberg in furious pursuit

splintering main group, and kept pace with the climbing cyclists until I found Patrice parked conveniently on the level road at the top. Sensing my urgency, made all the more obvious through my heavy breathing, Patrice took off once again into the maddening pace. Our target this time was just as demanding as before – to reach the Eikenberg ahead of the race. In the years when the Koppenberg had its place in the route, the photographers had but one option – to work there, and then take a large diversion around the race to arrive first at the Eikenberg, sure in the knowledge that it was impossible to get to the Taaienberg or Eikenberg with the race.

Since 1988 we've had to gamble on making it to the Eikenberg through a never-ending series of winding, narrow lanes, where the race has become even more broken than after the Patersberg. To add further complications, two small tarmacadam climbs – the Berg ten Houte and the Kouterberg – lie in the 14 kilometres between the Taaienberg and Eikenberg, each of them lined with thousands of cheering fans. It doesn't help

that live television coverage has now begun, and that a TV motorbike and a second helicopter have suddenly been added to the race. Knowing that after the Eikenberg a long stretch of open roads is unlikely to provide us with anything exciting, we soon get a feeling of paranoia as we all of us set about passing the shattered race at the first opportunity.

Some photographers squeezed past, but some didn't. It was our turn to nip past when the spectacular sight of the Berg Ten Houte came into view, bringing with it a warning from the official's car not to go by. While cursing this unwanted interference, I reluctantly told Patrice to hold off, having had one warning already from the officials; two warnings meant expulsion from the race. And that was that: no Eikenberg for us. For immediately the Berg Ten Houte began, someone up ahead attacked – a move that sparked a desperate pursuit between 20 men, each of them sensing this was the move to follow, each of them hell-bent on getting on board the non-stop express to glory. To add to my frustration while actually on the Eikenberg, I could

51

clearly see a few of my more fortunate colleagues photographing the action ahead of the racing. I could imagine the pictures they were getting of the 14-strong group that had emerged in the lanes around Schorisse, where the Eikenberg began.

By the time we'd overtaken the chasing group, which numbered perhaps 50, and had made it across to the leading riders, it had been nearly 30 kilometres since I'd last seen the front of a rider's face; but there was little to do there, as I now had to compose my thoughts for the impending climb of the Molenberg, with just 53 kilometres left. A familiar climb, having been in the route since 1983, the Molenberg offers a last opportunity to picture both breakaways and chasers, as there follows a welcome respite on main roads before the definitive climb of the Wall of Geraardsbergen. Having not put finger to shutter button for perhaps 20 minutes, I was anxious to rectify the situation on the Molenberg. The anxiety I'd first felt on the Patersberg, 40 kilometres earlier, had more than trebled by now.

My sight of the race was now impeded by the television motorbike of BRT, which hovered annoyingly just inches ahead of Dhaenens as he led the string of escapers up the cobbled slopes. I grabbed a wasted shot of the action, faring better with Peiper, who was clinging to the ferocious pace like a desperate sailor fleeing a sinking ship with his crew. This had been my first clear view of the break that had established itself after the Berg Ten Houte, and the characters escaping were an unlikely lot, with only one Flemish rider – Rudy Dhaenens – amongst them. Michel Dernies, a French-speaking Belgian, was there, but the rest were of a nationality that is normally unfamiliar at this stage in the 'Ronde'. Four Italians – Argentin, Giuseppe Calcaterra, Fondriest and the heroic Fabio Roscioli, who had until this point been alone way out in front all day – had infiltrated the break, aided by Peiper, Pedersen and Jarmann; Planckaert had dropped back on the Eikenberg.

That there wasn't one single Dutchman in the group

only added to the oddity of the day's racing – a feeling reinforced by the sight of Fignon, who was the next man to receive my attention on the Molenberg. I decided not to wait for the other chasers, and ran back up to Patrice, eager to follow Fignon to the head of the race.

As Fignon pounded on his pedals, so a growing entourage watched his every move, like me marvelling at his athleticism and courage. Helped partly by Dernies, who had punctured and dropped from the leaders, Fignon and his respectable entourage of three cars and six motorbikes drew up to the leaders as they approached the unpaved but strategic climb of the Berendries, with 31 kilometres now left. Not content with merely joining forces with the leaders, Fignon went straight by on the climb, duly photographed by the photographers from *L'Equipe* and *Het Nieuwsblad*, who at moments like this always seem to get away with ignoring officials' instructions and warnings! The rest of us had to wait until the moment had gone before being allowed past – a typically frustrating moment, especially as by the time we'd got by, Fignon had been pulled back.

But then luck came my way. No sooner had I got to the front of the group than Argentin launched his counter-attack, right in my viewfinder's sights. A quick few seconds of photography, and we pulled clear to let someone else take our privileged place. Next time I looked back, the white jersey of Dhaenens could be seen to the side of the Italian champion, and there was something in the way Argentin was riding that suggested the race could be almost over now. Still, our race radio told us that a large chasing group was only 40 seconds behind the splintered leaders, led by four of the Panasonic team.

Just two climbs to go now – the infamous Wall of Geraardsbergen (Mur de Grammont), and the smaller but equally definitive Bosberg. Even though we've touched 100 kilometres per hour for ten minutes, by the time we've dismounted and regained our equilibrium at the top of the hill, only a few minutes are left before the helicopter heralds the leaders' arrival

Edwig Van Hooydonck thrilled Belgium with his lone victory in 1989 . . .

. . . but Jacky Durand's surprise win in 1992 did little for the race's stature

in the picturesque town below. There are two places for photographers to stand here: on a sharp, 90-degree left-hand turn on the steepest of the cobbles, where the Omloop Het Volk is usually photographed; or further on, as the riders approach the summit in front of a small chapel, where Het Volk doesn't go.

Most of us choose the latter today, as it's closer to where our transport awaits, and affords us a better chance to get to the Bosberg before the race. Only a wet day would have persuaded us to go further down the climb, where so many memorable images have been captured on the most uneven and slippery cobblestones in the race, but from where it is nigh-on impossible to get back to the motorbikes quickly enough.

Almost before I've had time to collect my thoughts and choose my camera and lens combination, Argentin and Dhaenens race into view through the chicane formed by this curve in the routing, where their every gasp for breath is cheered by the thousands straddled across a grassy slope overlooking the whole scene. We're told a chasing group of six is now just 30 seconds behind, and all of us to a man await this potential threat to the leaders.

It is Fondriest who appears first, sprinting out of the saddle now that he knows he's in with a chance. Then it's our turn to sprint, Carl Lewis-style, back to the motorbikes, much to the amusement of the sun-drenched, beer-intoxicated crowd. We quit the hill in true desperado style, our crash helmets not yet placed on our heads, our cameras and jackets flapping in the wind as our drivers head off at maximum thrust. We rejoin the race route a few hundred metres behind the group containing Fondriest, and I curse at not having time to exploit the temporary absence of any policemen or officials. For we simply have to get to Dhaenens and Argentin, who by now are approaching the small hamlet of Moerbeke and the final climb of the day.

All the time, the race radio keeps us informed of the chasers now lining up behind the two leaders, guaranteeing a thrilling conclusion to the day. I choose to continue with the two leaders, whom we've now caught at the crossroads in the centre of the village, reasoning that I'll have time on the Bosberg itself to wait for Fondriest and still get to the finish on time. Patrice senses this too, remembering my detailed briefing to him earlier that day about what usually happens on the Bosberg. For many years now, this 500-metre-long hill has had the final say in the Tour of Flanders, launching stars like Merckx, Maertens, Raas, Van der Poel and Van Hooydonck to victory in Meerbeke, while destroying the efforts of men never destined to win 'De Ronde'.

An attack can be expected without fail, and anticipated here on the uneven cobbles. One year earlier, it had been Van Hooydonck who had attacked so successfully here, leaving five chasers in his wake, to head into Meerbeke for his first Tour of Flanders win – a movement captured only by the best photographers in the diabolical conditions that day. Today, however, was different, not just because of the sun, but because both men seemed happy to ride together to the finish, probably fearing that a lone attack would only help their chasers. While my colleagues hovered around the two men, bluntly ignoring officials' warnings, I directed Patrice to the top, sensing a better opportunity to be had there.

Selecting a spot most densely filled with wild fans, and wondering at their ability to re-find the race all day, I crouched down and awaited the leaders' arrival on the last climb, and the last cobbles, of the long race. Sure enough, Dhaenens and Argentin sped by together over the top of the climb, their motorbike entourage impressively chasing the crowd out of their path. I looked thoughtfully over my shoulder as they disappeared over the horizon, convinced I had made a better choice by waiting for Fondriest's group. No sooner had the last motorbike gone by than a policeman's motorbike escorting the chasers drove officiously through the crowds that had avidly reassembled there. I grabbed a clear – and I thought spectacular – shot of Fondriest. Teeth gritted, hands on the tops of his bars, shoulders bent with the effort, the Italian blasted by, followed inches away by equally grimacing men determined not to lose contact with their young locomotive.

Almost delirious that I had at last got a cracking shot, I jumped manicly onto the BMW, and Patrice fired us back into the race one final time, sensing the close proximity of the finish now less than twelve kilometres away. We stayed behind Fondriest's speeding chase as long as we dared, gaining a tantalising glimpse of the leaders a few hundred yards ahead on the road as it dropped into Ninove. We could also see a small set of chasers coming up fast from behind us. It was going to

be a close finish. I watched avidly as long as I dared, praying I might get one final shot if the leaders were caught. But eventually my nerve gave out, and I asked Patrice to take me to Meerbeke, I could not risk missing the finish of such an important race.

In any case, an awesome phalanx of motorbike police had already selected us out for special attention, so precariously balanced as the race was now. Using the worst French expletives, then the threat of physical persuasion, they did their job beyond perfection, but succeeded anyway in sending us away to the finish five kilometres down the road.

Before the imposition of officialdom and regulations in recent years, photographers used to enjoy this fast run to the finish, capturing precise moments when a race-winning move was launched, or when a potential move was foiled. In 1983 I was spellbound as Jan Raas attacked on this very road to achieve his second Flanders victory. Three years later it was Eric Vanderaerden, thrilling all of Flanders with his solo victory, while in 1986 I watched appalled as Sean Kelly gave Adrie Van der Poel an armchair ride to the finish, not realising the Dutchman had latched onto the three-man group that Kelly was towing to Meerbeke. In 1989 it was the turn of Van Hooydonck to pursuit to victory here, cheered and encouraged all the way by Eddy Merckx, who was happily employed for the day in the race organiser's yellow car. But 1988 was the year to remember – a brilliant duel between Eddy Planckaert and Phil Anderson that continued all the way to the finish line, with each rider relaying the other's attacks. All this has sadly ended now with the heavy burden of new regulations and we are obliged to leave for the finish well-ahead.

Today there was one obstacle for us still to overcome, even though we were a few minutes ahead of the race as we swung right into Meerbeke. In the excitement of the last half-hour, I'd forgotten the silly regulation that obliged us to take a small diversion five kilometres from the finish – a diversion we'd long since overshot.

Expecting the worst, I instructed Patrice to repeat his tactic of the Patersberg. Right on cue, a flag-waving official moved to block our path as we swung into the Hallebaan. At first he waved at us; then, realising that we were determined to get by, he lunged at my still-open jacket. Our 1000 ccs of wonderful German engineering won the day, and we powered victoriously to the finish line, leaving an irate official to his fate; I'd grabbed his flag when he grabbed my jacket.

As it turned out, the finish was something of an anticlimax, for once Argentin and Dhaenens had been sighted turning through that same corner, unchallenged by the flagless official, we knew they would not be caught. We also knew that the Italian would win easily – which he did by three lengths. The determined Fondriest had come in fifth, failing by just 14 seconds to catch his compatriot; but his efforts would not have gone unacknowledged in this cycling-mad country. No sooner had Fondriest's group crossed the line than the road quickly filled with thousands of half-drunk bike fans and it was a relief to retire to a quieter spot a few hundred metres beyond the line, where photographers and drivers exchanged their stories of the 1990 Ronde van Vlaanderen, and of the places where it all went wrong!

With the bars and cafés of this little village now filling to bursting point with race fans, it's time to move on. Already the roads around the finish are choc-a-bloc with cars and cyclists heading home, and we too slip onto the highway towards Brussels, swapping the privileges that being in 'De Ronde' have given us for a more restrained mode of driving.

The Tour of Flanders is a fantastic race, for cyclists, photographers and fans alike. It is maddeningly frustrating, when that special piece of action remains so elusive in the hectic environment. I cannot ever recall being satisfied at the end of a 'Ronde', it is this challenge that brings me back year after year to St Niklaas, and to each of the 13 special hills – I wouldn't want to miss it for all the world.

ADRIE VAN DER POEL

6 April 1986: Tour of Flanders

The road from the Bosberg to Meerbeke is more than ten kilometres long – long enough and wide enough to afford a clear view behind the three-man breakaway as it headed flat-out for the finish of the Tour of Flanders. For Jean-Philippe Vandenbrande and Steve Bauer, but most especially for Sean Kelly, this rolling highway represented the final leg of one of the greatest prizes in professional cycling – a win in 'De Ronde'.

The three had come together during the course of the last ten kilometres: first Vandenbrande and Kelly had pooled their strengths to clear the Muur van Geraardsbergen ahead of their colleagues in the day's only important breakaway; then they had caught the Canadian, Bauer, at the foot of the Bosberg, the final climb in the race. And now they rode, three men as one, uniting to maintain a slender lead of just 15 seconds. It was Kelly who worked the hardest, as the Irishman always does in these daring last-ditch efforts. Kelly pedalled his muscular legs for all they're worth, pumping hard on his highest gear to keep the break's momentum going, all the time squirming around in his saddle to see the situation behind.

If he'd had the time to take in the chasing figure accurately, Kelly might well have eased up as the break approached the last eight kilometres, the urban build-up of houses now a startling indication of the riders' close proximity to the finish. The lone figure grew ever closer, then latched onto the rear of the group as Kelly continued powering away at the front – oblivious, it seemed, to the danger behind – or perhaps uncaring of it. Only on the last undulation before the drop into Meerbeke did Kelly give the cyclist a long hard look, and seemed shocked to see who in fact it was: Dutchman Adrie Van der Poel, the most exciting cyclist to have emerged from the Netherlands in years.

Kelly's pained look as he recognised Van der Poel at the back was the last thing I saw before quitting the race for the finish, and it was then I knew that Kelly faced losing the race. At the finish, Van der Poel – fresher than the Irishman, having joined late and not worked with the

breakaway – came off Kelly's wheel with 75 metres remaining to score the best win of his career. Kelly, although second, was punished for his carelessness at such a crucial part in the race. For had he not worked so hard once Van der Poel had latched on, he might surely have won the only 'true' classic that had eluded him then, and still does today.

ERIC VANDERAERDEN

12 APRIL 1987: PARIS–ROUBAIX

The figure bouncing towards me was unmistakable, all blond tenacity and acrobatics as he wiggled his bike over the slick, muddy surface of the road. There were no cobblestones at this point – instead just a soft-packed surface of brown mud and motorcar tyre tracks. Eric Vanderaerden was a sight to behold as he took the cobbled section of the Paris–Roubaix horror in his stride, never compromising his speed for safety as he chased the three breakaways still more than a minute ahead. I'd arrived late at this spot near to Camphin-en-Pévèle, and had missed the trio of Rudy Dhaenens, Patrick Versluys and Jean-Philippe as they'd striven to maintain a lead that had been established just 20 kilometres into the race.

I had photographed a fourth member of that breakaway, Theo de Rooy, as he crashed into the same ground that Vanderaerden was now cruising over, and over which a few minutes later Sean Kelly would ride ever so gently, having crashed a few kilometres further back. The day's result belonged to Vanderaerden – I had no doubt – and we took off in pursuit as soon as Kelly's timid, mud-stained arrival confirmed Vanderaerden's successful escape from the Irishman.

I next saw the race near to Hem, as first Versluys, then Vandenbrande, then Dhaenens rode past, their triumvirate broken apart by crashes on the last sections of *pavé*. Then when I saw Vanderaerden, my adrenalin pumped – he was going to win! Not waiting for any more chasers, I leapt back on my driver's bike, willing him to take off into the race even without official accreditation.

We drew up behind Vanderaerden as he steadily gained ground on the trio now belatedly rejoined in their attack. But it was no contest: metre by metre, kilometre by kilometre, the hero of all Belgium drew ever closer. Finally making contact on the outskirts of Roubaix itself, his tucked-elbow style and rocking shoulders was simply breathtaking as he piled on the pressure to invalidate the breakaways' long escape. My driver couldn't refuse me now, not now, and I implored him to overtake the breakaway before the finish – an act he carried out under sincere emotional pressure. My hero Vanderaerden was going to win the Paris–Roubaix; nobody was going to deny me this poignant image! And win he did, with ease, with style, with class – the way he'd won the 1985 Tour of Flanders, the way I hoped he'd win many more classics.

Jean-Marie Wampers and Eddie Planckaert were first into the Wallers-Arenberg forest in 1990

PARIS-ROUBAIX

It was one o'clock in the morning, and less than nine hours to the start of the Paris–Roubaix. Both of us were tired from two days of concentrated preparation for the coming day – tired from an evening-long search for hotel rooms, and from a slow evening meal in the ancient city of Compiègne, 30 kilometres away. Yet that afternoon had been by far the most stressful episode of the past two days – the unknown fate as to whether I would be allowed into the world's greatest one-day race on a motorbike.

The previous week I had been making frantic phonecalls from Brussels, first to a friend near Turin, and then for the second time to the Société du Tour de France's offices in Paris, in order to establish whether an Italian photographer was actually coming to Paris–Roubaix. 'It's very simple', I'd been told by the race's *Chef de Presse*, Philippe Sudres. 'If Sergio Penazzo doesn't come, you're in the race.' That had been after the previous weekend's Tour of Flanders, when the Italian photographer hadn't turned up, and my calls to a friend in Italy had been to determine whether he would be taking his allocation for Paris–Roubaix.

By Thursday, I'd received the news I'd hoped for: Penazzo wasn't coming, claiming to Sudres that he was ill. I knew the reason was more material: only one noted Italian, Franco Ballerini, was competing, and that simply made the race too much of a gamble to induce Penazzo to travel from his Milan base. Fondriest, Argentin and Bugno had all declined to participate – and I'd taken a sudden liking to Italian cyclists! But my anxiety hadn't ended there. Having been told by Sudres in March that there wasn't likely to be a place for me in the photographers' entry, which was limited to 13, I'd made no plans to bring my trusted *motard*, Patrice, up from his home near Cannes, knowing in any case that this distinguished driver had little interest in driving me on a series of detours around the race.

So it was I found myself sharing a room this night with an English driver, Luke Evans, whose only previous experience of continental race driving had been four days in that year's Paris–Nice stage race. When Luke had initially said yes, it had been in the belief that we'd be out of the race, making a series of diversions to get around the race. That had all changed three days before Paris–Roubaix, following a final call to Sudres in Paris; so Luke had bravely agreed to drive me in the Paris–Roubaix, and had also agreed to spend a day and a half on a reconnoitre of every single cobbled section on the whole course. The only remaining doubts had been whether Sudres would give me the all-important green 'plaque' as he'd promised – and then whether he'd remember that Luke had worked as a journalist on the previous year's Tour de France!

If there's one race guaranteed to test the mettle of a photographer's driver it is Paris–Roubaix. Whether on dry roads or wet, this crazy race demands the utmost in skill and concentration from everyone in the race, and I fell into a very light sleep that night, praying Luke was up to the challenge. Less than six hours later we were back in Compiègne for the start. The promised fine day hadn't yet materialised; outside the skies were leaden with heavy grey cloud. A few drops of rain fell onto the motorbike as Luke lovingly re-oiled its chain in anticipation of the battering to come, and I felt a strange sense of guilt that I was about to subject him and his red-and-white Honda to a baptism of fire. Usually before a Paris–Roubaix I silently pray for early morning rain to transform the course into a quagmire – and therefore a photographer's delight. On this morning, I prayed otherwise.

There was barely 50 minutes to the start, and I lost 15 of those precious minutes searching for a car that would take our baggage. Not wishing to subject Luke to the bustle of the race leaving town on the wet cobblestones, I elected to get away a few minutes ahead, wary of the drops of rain still falling cruelly from the sky. We drove on way ahead of the race, passing the

No guessing why the photographers stand here every year: these riders have to bunny-hop over the holes in the road through the Wallers-Arenberg Forest

It's harder to bunny-hop over the holes in the wet, which is why so many photographers are camped here

advance convoy of press cars heading for an early lunch. In a race so full of drama and excitement, the early kilometres are a strange experience – a reality almost detached from the ordeal to come. Passing out of Compiègne, we follow the yellow routing signs so distinctive in the quiet of the morning, and disappear into a 10-kilometre-long corridor through dense forest, where the odour of chopped wood mingles with the damp atmosphere to bring a chill to your body. It's quiet now – too quiet perhaps – but I exploit the silence to collect my thoughts on how I'm going to steer Luke through his apprenticeship in the Hell of the North, and at the same time come back with a vast stock of memorable images.

Every year since 1987, the race has encountered its first cobblestones at Troisvilles, a sleepy village lying in the farmlands to the south of Cambrai. In Troisvilles,

the race enters hell on a left fork in the road to Neuilly immediately dumping the riders into a water-filled trench on the first cobbles, then dropping into a small valley, a 90-degree left-hand bend and a gradually rising track which leads into the heart of the fields.

It was at a crossroads somewhere in this nowhere land that Luke and I now stood. We'd followed almost every kilometre of cobbles during the previous two days, but had left this section to be checked out today before the race arrived. To satisfy our final curiosity, Luke duly tracked the path to its end in someone's farmyard in the village of Viesly.

Happy to have finished our reconnoitre, we went back to Troisvilles for refreshment and a complete analysis of what we were planning to do, taking the opportunity *en route* to try a shaky looking track as a possible detour when the race arrived. Two things at least seemed sure about the day: first I would be a nervous wreck worrying about Luke and the race itself, and second it would be dry. It had been weeks since any rain had fallen in this part of France, and even as we stood, with more than an hour to wait before the race arrived, the sun was already burning off the haze and warming us in the fields.

On paper the plan was simple: to make deliberate diversions around the race as far as the feeding station in Valenciennes, then to stay in the race all the way to Roubaix. That way, I reasoned, we'd stay out of trouble in the earlier sections when little of note would happen in the dry conditions anyway, then really go to work as the race began to break up. I also knew my own commitment to my work. Once the real racing began, my demands on Luke would be no less than if they were being directed to a more experienced driver; I'd expect Luke to go into any situation required of him. Only my tolerance would be extended today, should Luke get into difficulties – but I began to curse myself for being so full of doubt. We were going to have a good day.

I chose to await the race at the crossroads, about two kilometres into the first cobbled section – there being 22 so designated sections in the race. As we waited, people in ones or twos, in cars, on bicycles, and on foot, began to emerge right out of the fields. These were locals, brought up in the very backyard of the Hell of the North, and therefore so familiar with the landscape as to be able to target the best places to see the race. And our spot did look good, coming after the first cobbles that would have caused some damage to the peloton already. We waited still, and I began to fiddle with the race radio, urging it to work on such an important day, for by now we should be well within radio contact of the approaching race. But something was wrong: either I'd programmed the wrong frequency into the receiver, or the battering it had sustained in the previous weekend's race had damaged something. I grew anxious of the implications.

By now the crowd had swelled to a few hundred, and everyone clung to the edges of the track for the best vantage point, covering their eyes to avoid the dirt being thrown up by the advance press cars now clattering along the cobbles; it wouldn't be long now. I gleaned from a spectator's radio that an eleven-strong group was about five minutes ahead of the main field, just five kilometres from Troisvilles. Press cars continued to arrive, and I spotted familiar faces in the seats – faces staring at this strange world outside, so laughably removed from the harsh realities that our Paris–Roubaix would present us with. But I envied them not – the best television coverage in the world could never match actually being there.

More cars, and now motorbikes; many of my colleagues had also sought out this same spot. I took a silly pride in having got here first, and engaged one Belgian photographer in anxious conversation: 'What's been happening?' I asked – but like me he'd not yet encountered the race since Compiègne, and could offer no clues as to what to expect. I made a mental note of his expression: did I look that nervous too? The distant sound of a helicopter could be heard, even above the clattering of car tyres on cobbles – any moment now. Over the hill a dust cloud loomed large. Soon the silhouettes of gendarmes' motorbikes could be seen emerging from the cloud. On their heels came one official's motorbike, and then at last, at last, a cyclist. Then came more, but they were just dark shadows completely indistinguishable in the dust.

I crouched on the inside of our corner, taking grabbed shots with a wide-angle lens whenever I was sure I was in focus. No award-winning shots were to be had here – that I knew – but I continued firing, enjoying the chance at last to photograph something of the action. Within a few seconds the first group had passed through, and soon the dust began to settle again, making life more bearable for everyone there. But not for long – the five-minute gap was obviously being shortened. Over the hill, a new cloud of dust began to rise, barely three minutes since the group had passed through. Still in the

Whether on cobblestones or mountain passes, Laurent Fignon is a favourite subject. Here he chased hard after puncturing during the 1989 Paris–Roubaix

Stephen Roche left a puncture victim behind at Wallers-Arenberg in 1983

same place as before, I fired off a long series of shots, occasionally sighting a familiar face in my viewfinder, but invariably shooting at nothing, for in these dry conditions there really was nothing yet to be had.

As the stragglers began to file past in the thick cloud of dust that now enveloped us, I shouted for Luke to get ready – already my colleagues were accelerating into the back of the race. But we opted for the shaky detour that we'd tried out 30 minutes earlier, reasoning we would make it ahead of the main group before Viesly – maybe even get ahead of the eleven riders in front. A few minutes later, we found ourselves behind the eleven, having successfully negotiated the detour. Rather than hang about here, though, we accelerated past on the next available stretch of tarmac in search of a decent cobbled section. My confidence in Luke began to grow, and thank goodness it was dry!

Within five kilometres we pulled up on a short rise, halfway along the fourth section in the race. Once we had worked here, we'd divert again to a familiar point in the field that is – normally – under inches of water. The eleven pounded by, led by Belgium's Johan Capiot, and I chose to await the main group here in the fields, knowing we could easily get around them later. The gap was now less than two minutes as a nearly complete peloton rode steadily by us. Again I shot off a load of frames, but again I knew I was just going through the motions, for there was little in the way of excitement. We drove off as soon as a suitable gap appeared in the fragmenting tail-end of the large, strung-out group.

Luke seemed completely at home in his strange environment, I began to regret that it was so dry – maybe he could have handled wet conditions just as well. The race emerged onto the main road to Valenciennes after a few more kilometres in the fields, minus a dozen or so riders who had punctured on this latest section of *pavé*. Yet still it was a larger group than we normally see by this point, and I grew ever more anxious about the outcome of the race. We drove peacefully at the back of the peloton as it reached the first feeding station in Solesmes, with my colleagues respectfully allowing Luke his elected place in the single file of photographers' bikes; we were just two bikes from the back of the peloton.

From my pillion seat I detected an air of growing confidence as he accelerated through the meandering bends along the road, seeking out the next diversion for us to make into the fields in order to get to a favoured location before the eleven escapers. Though it meant

missing a large chunk of *pavé* to get there, I was excited about the next stop, recalling previous years' adventures there when it wasn't quite so dry. There was no water on the cobbles today – just a bone-dry crater that had once held water in this dip in the landscape. I was disappointed, although I tried not to show it so early in the race.

There was little time to reflect, for already the breakaway group was entering the *pavé* two kilometres from where we waited. Other photographers pulled up now, surprised to see me already waiting there; they too expressed disappointment at the 'unsporting' conditions. Capiot again was leading the escapers, riding with great spirit a few metres ahead of the others as he

This television reporter's motorbike came a cropper in the 1985 race

bounded through the shallow crater. Yet already in the distance I could see the dust clouds that indicated the main group's progress onto these same cobbles. From here on, the serious stuff was about to begin, and I grew anxious once again, nervous of the unphotogenic conditions and of the challenge Luke now faced as we approached the real hell.

We moved off into the back of the still fragmenting peloton on this, the most narrow stretch of *pavé* in the entire race. I'd briefed Luke on the difficulties of this particular section, where it was often necessary to drive on the grass in order to keep clear of the team cars and the riders dangling between the cars. And it was dusty – so dusty that it was impossible to see further than the car now driving a few inches ahead of Luke's front wheel.

As we bounced and rattled our way along this four-kilometre stretch of cobbles, I reflected that so far I hadn't seen one crash – not even a small one. I recognised a ditch on our right that an RMO rider had fallen into last year, causing a major blockage in the scramble to retrieve him. But this year there was nothing – only the dust, the dirt and the sun. We sped down a descent, now nearing the end of the *pavé*, and exited through a sharp right-hand bend to join the main road to Valenciennes again. It seemed strange to feel tarmacadam under our wheels after ten minutes or more of a bruising ride. Just 15 kilometres and the second feeding station separated us from our rendezvous with the feared Wallers-Arenberg forest.

The Capiot-led group was in sight of the chasers at the entry to Valenciennes, but race director Jean-Marie Leblanc allowed us to overtake anyway, respecting the photographers' needs to get well ahead for the coming spectacular. Two kilometres from the forest, we're directed off the highway towards the hamlet of Arenberg, a former mining settlement whose brightly painted houses now reflect the changing times. At the entry to the forest, a massive winding-gear structure stands idle, adding an aura of foreboding to the environment. And actually on the first cobbles, we pass under a tall railway bridge, whose rails used to carry tons of coal from the nearby colliery.

This is it – the most notorious section of *pavé* in the legend of Paris–Roubaix. Two days ago the forest seemed the most tranquil place on earth when we made a brief 'recky' – not a soul to be seen, only the twittering and singing of the permanent inhabitants of this bird sanctuary in the tall trees above. Today it is a human-infested swamp – but dry. Thousands upon thousands of people are crammed into the forest, spread two-deep along the section's entire three-kilometre length, each and every one of them having carefully selected their own particular spot where they believe one or another rider will fall at their very feet. From the railway bridge, the track noticeably drops into the depths of the forest, ensuring a high-speed start, before levelling out 500 metres in. It is here that we are all gathered, sensing – even relishing – some incident or another in an area where large chunks of cobblestones are missing, and where a cyclist's front wheel can so easily become dislodged by hitting a hole at 50 kilometres per hour. The spectators stand five-deep here.

The 15-minute cushion we've gained since we last saw the race is a godsend, and I take the time to talk Luke through the next phase of the course, and to consider our plans from this point on. So far I've been impressed with his driving, and I wonder why I've been so anxious at this morning's start. But the real test is about to begin, and as dry and comparatively easy as the conditions are today, I can't help recalling Patrice's nonchalant skills in this forest last year when we'd tracked the leading riders all the way to the end of the path, ours being the only bike in that position on the slippery cobblestones. I'd never doubted my good fortune in teaming up with Patrice that year, for in 1989 he had driven an ABC cameraman down that same path, actually *leading* the riders in conditions far removed from today's. The images his cameraman filmed were to win both of them a share of an Emmy prize for that

year's footage of Paris–Roubaix on the American screens.

But today is a day slowly filling with adventures that would be only ours, for nobody outside this prestigious clique could possibly begin to appreciate its subtleties, let alone its excitement and danger. The crowd all around us was abuzz with anticipation of the drama waiting to unfold. From this point on in the race, all the cobbled sections would be lined with tens of thousands of crazed fans, most of them Belgians from across the nearby border, chafing at the bit to see their skilled countrymen secure yet another victory in Paris– Roubaix. Last year it had been Eddy Planckaert, the year before Jean-Marie Wampers, the year before that Dirk De Mol. Who knew which of them would win this year?

The race began to arrive, at least in the mining village beyond the entry to the forest, and the crowd grew yet more expectant. It's a precarious location is ours, crouched on the cobbles so dangerously close to the oncoming cyclists, all the time fending off the pushes and shoves from enthusiastic spectators craning their necks for a clear view from behind. A convoy of red official cars batters past, centimetres from our knees and elbows, followed instantly by gendarmes' motorbikes determined to carve a safe path through this human mass for the athletes behind. Then come the heroes themselves, so fearless of the impending peril as the speed of their descent drops them onto the decimating cobblestones. But there's still no crash – not even here.

I'm positioned right at the edge of the cobbles, my reactions shared equally between getting scenes of the action as the riders bunny-hop the crater, and occasionally jumping out of the way as one or two riders opt for a softer ride exactly where I'm standing. But it's all too quick, too rushed, this long-savoured dash across the Wallers-Arenberg forest. Where on previous occasions riders have disappeared into the woods or tumbled into hapless spectators, so fast were they going on a wet path, today everyone to a man keeps his

Rolf Sörensen fighting hard near Attiches in 1991 . . .

balance, and the main body of the race has already pounded by when I realise there's little left to photograph.

We drive off onto the famous cobbles, but already spectators begin filling the road as the end of the main group has now gone by, and the path-clearing team cars are yet to arrive. The Buckler team car arrives hurriedly behind us, and I suggest to Luke that he lets the car past so we can have an easier ride through to the end of the forest – a hint quickly accepted as more cars approach from behind. The driver of the Buckler car is none other than Jan Raas, himself a winner of Paris–Roubaix in 1982.

I remember 1986, when Sean Kelly led the race onto the forest's cobbles – his eyes had a special look – and it was no surprise when he arrived first in Roubaix that day. Instantly I regret Kelly's absence today due to injury, realising too that it has been two years now since Kelly last graced the Hell of the North. The race misses

this two-time winner, for Paris–Roubaix is all about its former victors – the most heroic and swashbuckling of all classics' winners.

Within five minutes, we've reached the end of the Wallers-Arenberg forest – the end of that wall of thousands – and join in the mad scramble of cars, motorbikes and cyclists, all trying to regroup after the damage of the cobbles. We race past each group of cyclists, frantically chasing to get back to the head of the race. I slow Luke up as we pass a group led by Martial Gayant and Laurent Fignon, just long enough to get a few shots of the two French favourites; on a day as dry as this, Fignon might just achieve his ambition of winning Paris–Roubaix after all.

We return to cobbles once more, though only for 500 metres. On reaching tarmacadam Luke accelerates into the group to get ahead for the next sections. We're halfway down the group of 120 cyclists that's racing flat-out to maintain its advantages over any stragglers,

. . . as Greg LeMond chases in vain a few seconds later

including Fignon. But just as soon as we see clear road ahead of us, so a sharp swerve amidst the peloton pushes us hard against the left kerb to leave us trapped inside the violent energy of the hungry pack. Luke keeps his place and his nerve, waiting cannily for another opportunity to pass. I glance behind us: nobody has tried following us through – a further sign of Luke's mushrooming skills. Eventually we make it through, and I slap Luke on the back in recognition of his work. Yes, I wish now that it had rained.

A break began to develop in the twisty lanes between Hornaing and Wandignies-Hamage, containing Englishman Sean Yates, Frenchman Charly Mottet, Hendrik Redant and two other Belgians, and Dutchman Nico Verhoeven. Lifted by seeing Yates in this good move, we stayed with the six as they crossed section after section of cobbles, only waiting for the main group once, on the wide road to Orchies where it would be easy to pass.

As the race left Orchies, I was already in place on the bridge, photographing first the break containing Yates, then a minute later the massive peloton. As I focused down on the colourful mass snaking its way onto the winding track, I made a quick assessment of its size: perhaps 100 riders were in there together, an unprecedented number still in with a chance at this stage. I'd stood on this bridge in 1986, the year Kelly had won, and recalled taking a similar picture when the group numbered barely 20!

We made a worthwhile diversion to intersect the race before it emerged from those same cobbles. Then came a long series of cobbled tracks that would deliver the surviving riders into the last, and worst, cobbled sections of the race.

On our next diversion, we emerged along the side of a farmhouse onto some favoured cobbles that would – normally – be submerged in brown, muddy water. Today they seemed so uninteresting – just dirt and stones – and I chose to stay ahead to find a better location on a strategic uphill section near Attiches. But we were

barely ahead of the leaders as we approached our next location, the section of *pavé* before the hill – and too good to miss. Yates hove into view, hauling Mottet and Redant along in his wake, determined to make the best of this situation for his team-mate Steve Bauer.

Quickly the main group followed, less than 30 seconds behind now; they'd soon be caught. With the sun's strong rays lighting the scene we stayed to shoot the main group, using a long 300mm lens to emphasise the collective strength this group possessed. But even as I focused on Bauer and Jean-Claude Collotti in the front line, I realised that I'd made Luke's job that much harder to get to the uphill section in time. We followed a regrouped peloton down a long, dropping section of cobbles and I remembered a diversion I'd had to make two years before at the end of this track: maybe, just maybe, I could get us around it.

A race official directed the following convoy down the route, into a 90-degree right-hand turn at the end of the track. But I shouted at Luke to go straight ahead there, and he drove as fast as the conditions allowed to the main road above, making a hasty right turn when instructed, and speeding me all the way to where I knew the cobbled hill joined the road we now travelled on. I ran from the bike, inspired on sensing the television helicopter had not yet reached us. I made it to the cobbles just in time to photograph Yates and Mottet as they bounded into view, thrilled at having got to this particular spot. Behind the two remaining leaders the race had exploded, and my adrenalin raced in the excitement of what I was seeing.

Franco Ballerini had attacked on the hill, devastating the main group that was now spread out all over the cobbles. The big Italian sped by with a cluster of men hanging on; then came Van Hooydonck with his cluster of followers, and finally Rolf Sörensen, so vivid in his white World Cup leader's jersey. Sörensen was struggling: for sure, he wouldn't make this decisive selection. A few minutes passed before Greg LeMond appeared, his distinctive front forks clearly of little help

74

to him now as his shoulders rolled under the fatigue his body was enduring. I'd waited as long as I dared here, determined to capitalise on this explosion in the race, very much aware that it was my last chance to photograph any of the weakening riders.

By the time we caught the leaders up, the riders who had attacked on the hill were as one, and I counted them to be seven, including Allan Peiper, who was having a great race today. We followed them onto the next cobbles near Seclin, a small town nudging the perimeter of Lille's international airport. Almost immediately Peiper punctured, and I shouted at Luke to stop, I was determined to record at least one incident of note today; so far the race had been completely without.

The likeable Australian wasted no time in getting back to the race, Peiper retook his place in the magnificent seven as they pounded flat-out down three kilometres of *pavé*. Standing up behind Luke, I relished the poignant scene as the seven men threw in their lot, on this cobbled road in the fields. But I wanted to get in front to record their expressions, sensing these men were riding to their absolute limit in an effort to finalise the race's destiny; a chasing group was just a few hundred metres behind. Luke drove down the left side, the first of five motorbikes hoping to slip past on this extra-narrow section. We almost made it, but then Ballerini chose that very instant to switch to the left, riding now on the same stretch of grass as we were, while forcing his rivals to persist on the bone-jarring cobbles.

Sensing the delicacy of the moment I became hyper-nervous: Luke, driving in only his second big race, was now just inches behind a cycling superstar, with only an inch or two of grass separating us from a deep ditch to our left. I was still standing up behind Luke, and seemed transfixed by the motion of Ballerini's huge torso and extravagant leg muscles directly in front. To our right rode six equally great men, while behind a cacophony of horns from cars and motorbikes sounded the warning that the chasing group was closing fast. Oblivious to the mounting pressure from behind, Luke seemed hell-bent

on getting past Ballerini, no matter how determinedly the Italian hogged his treasured terrain, while technical director Albert Bouvet watched our every move with severe scrutiny. Something had to give, and I knew it wouldn't be Ballerini – I just hoped it wouldn't be Luke's nerve.

Sensing an imminent explosion from Bouvet, who was travelling slightly behind us in his red car, I persuaded Luke to pull up at a small patch of ground I'd spotted a hundred metres in front, and his skidding halt in the dirt was imitated by the other bikes behind us. Just seconds after we stopped, a group of 18 riders flashed past to latch onto the group ahead. If we'd been caught up in their action, I'd have had some explaining to do later. In the town of Ennetières we chanced our luck again, getting past easily this time in the town's main street, and I banged off a few shots of the newly formed group, incredulous at how such a hard-working group of seven could get caught in full flight – the race was far from over.

Another landmark in the route was looming closer: the set of cobbles near the village of Ennevlin that had been Kelly's downfall twice in recent years. Still driving impeccably, Luke sped off down the road, turning left into the 17th cobbled section of the day. After two more kilometres, a race official tried to direct us away from the race route onto the diversion for all press cars, so bad were the cobbles we were about to encounter. But I was having none of that – not now, not in a race so lacking in drama. I needed the spectacle the next cobblestones had always given me in the past, and told Luke to drive right past the man; we left his curses hanging in the warm air as we accelerated away.

My disappointment was far from over, however, for as soon as we turned left into what had once passed as a road 200 years ago but was now a series of dry holes in the ground, I knew today's race had lost its last chance of drama: there would be no crashes here in Ennevlin. As I squatted in the left-hand ditch, normally filled with oozing brown mud, my mind raced back to

The attack that almost won him the 1990 Paris–Roubaix: Steve Bauer drags Eddy Planckaert and Edwig Van Hooydonck away at Carrefour de l'Arbe

the previous years I'd been here – to the slithering chaos of 1988, when Kelly fell; and to 1989, when Fignon too came a cropper in the mud. In its present dry state it seemed so vacant, so lifeless, though I doubt any of the cyclists now heading this way would have agreed. The race was almost upon us, and I looked beyond our corner in the road and across the fields to where the 25-strong group now approached.

Van der Poel was leading the charge for pole position at our corner, and the Dutchman flashed through my sights with Planckaert at his side, each man making a mockery of the easy conditions here. Not one of the leaders fell or so much as stumbled here, and I cursed through my laboured breathing as I ran the 50 yards back to Luke's bike. We sped on again, soon within sight

of the leading group, which seemed under pressure from the number of riders still in contention. I watched from behind as Redant, who had been away earlier with Yates and Mottet, sped off on his own in an attempt to take the race on. Behind him, riders from the Panasonic team were too busy watching other teams' riders to worry about Redant. Once his lead had gone past 20 seconds, we overtook to see what it was all about, then went off in the direction of Cysoing to the start of the next cobbles. Arriving five minutes before Redant, Luke pushed his bike through the thick crowd into our escape road beyond. Strictly speaking, the dry conditions were such that we could have stayed on the race route, but this diversion had always done me well in the past and I chose loyalty over change.

Marc Madiot's acceleration at Carrefour de l'Arbe led him to victory in 1991

Other photographers arrived, their faces reflecting the same disillusionment that I felt too, and I doubted whether my face was any cleaner than theirs. Most of us found a few seconds' amusement when a Belgian photographer began a punch-up with an angry spectator (the man resented us obscuring his view of the race). I pitied the spectator, although I couldn't understand any of the Flemish insults he was shouting into the photographer's face. The rotund man quickly dropped his cause when he heard Redant was away on his own, and a few seconds later the giant Belgian cyclist careered round the corner, caught in a blaze of flashlights from the dozen photographers crouched low out of the spectators' view.

Twenty-five seconds passed before three more cyclists arrived, led by another Belgian, Peter De Clercq. With hindsight, I made the wrong choice as I grabbed a shot of the third man, Wilfred Peeters, ignoring the tongue-out expression of Marc Madiot – 'Well, he hasn't won anything for years', I remember thinking then.

When Madiot arrived first at the junction and at the head of what was now a five-man leading group, I knew something had happened to Redant since I'd photographed his escape just minutes earlier, and cursed having chosen to take the diversion. With Ballerini as one of the five, I wanted to follow but fumbled to put the 300 mm lens away. We eventually accelerated away, passing an angry-looking Redant, who was chasing hard to recover from an untimely puncture.

Now on good roads we pulled alongside the five leaders, and I took note of who was there as I composed my photograph: Madiot led Ballerini, John Talen, De Clercq and Peeters, each of them rotating quickly in the stiff crosswind. It looked serious now, but it was anybody's guess as to which of these five would make it to Roubaix first. I put my money on Ballerini, in respect of the lone chase he'd successfully made to join Madiot's group.

So confident was I of Luke's skills, and of the uncertainty of the race at this time, that I elected to stay close to the leaders, digging deep into my sagging morale in the hope of snapping the race-winning attack. We stayed in front as the group began the 19th section of *pavé*, but I pulled Luke back closer to the riders when De Clercq raised the pace, wanting a shot of every move that happened. Only now did I not regret the lack of radio contact with the race – the officials could say all they wanted to me, but I had no way of hearing them! De Clercq's attack came to nothing, and we accelerated clear for a few seconds, my belief in Ballerini swelled by the sight of his yellow Del Tongo jersey through the thick dust clouds.

The group was surrounded by motorbikes, perhaps 15 of them: TV cameramen, officials, radio commentators and photographers, all poised for the next three kilometres of *pavé* that had to inspire the winning attack. The cobbled track swung right at a 90-degree turn, and I asked Luke to pull onto the grass in anticipation of any attack coming out of the bend. Ballerini sprinted out of the corner – Luke tried to accelerate from his spot on the grass, but made a hash of it, forgetting the soft, dirt surface. His back wheel spun, the bike slewed sideways. I momentarily closed my eyes, not wanting to see the collision as Ballerini closed in on us, but Luke regained control, flicking his light bike in a straight line once again. I too regained some composure, focusing on Ballerini's ever-passive

face as the Italian raced five feet behind our bike; I could imagine Bouvet turning purple in rage at our carelessness!

I was now expecting a repeat performance of last year's exciting finale, when Steve Bauer and Eddy Planckaert attacked out of a dead turn to the left with one kilometre of these cobbles still left. I noticed a few of my colleagues already on that corner now, expecting that the attack would have already come by the time the leaders arrived there. But I chose to go further ahead to the ensuing straight stretch of cobbles, as this would give us greater freedom of movement if the bulk of photographers was static on that bend. Feeling noticeably jaded now after a long day, I did my best to explain my needs to Luke as clearly as possible: we had to get alongside whoever attacked here, regardless of television, officials' warnings and my colleagues' similar ambitions.

I looked behind me, down the track lined edge-to-edge with thousands of people, and glimpsed a white jersey alone in the dust clouds. It could have been Ballerini's yellow jersey, but I knew Madiot's distinctive style. I grew tense, informing Luke of what was happening, though certain by now that he must have lost all track of where he was and what he was doing. Madiot drew closer, riding in the dirt on the left side of the track. Luke continued to hover slowly along the right-hand edge of the track, while behind I could see Ballerini chasing hard, still just a few feet from Madiot's rear wheel. Behind him came a phalanx of cars and motorbikes, now trapped behind the leaders. Luke accelerated, urged on by me to capitalise on this strategic move. I didn't care about the arm-waving officials I could see stuck behind the strung-out attack; I didn't care about the close proximity of the *Antenne 2* television motorbike; I only cared about whether Luke could match his speed with that of Madiot's, just long enough for me to do my work. I fired off about 20 frames in a rush of adrenalin, cock-a-hoop about the way my fortune had turned. It had been a long, frustrating day,

The apocalyptic figures of Sean Kelly and Marc Madiot in in 1983

A famous victory: Dirk de Mol wins the 1988 Paris–Roubaix

but now I put all that behind me as I gleefully swapped my colour camera for the black-and-white one – this moment was too good to miss! Out of the corner of my left eye I saw *L'Equipe's* motorbike, which had somehow joined us from behind, but Luke kept me with Madiot's acceleration all the way to the end of the cobbles, our freedom jeopardised only by the television motorbike and Jacques Garcia's red BMW. I wondered what the master thought of my rookie driver's ability.

We pulled away on the 200 metres of tarmac that separated us from the next section of cobbles – the 21st – and hovered a few hundred metres down, not wishing to overstay our welcome at the side of Madiot; I looked back at the race, to where my other colleagues had now joined the rush to photograph Madiot on his own – still smiling at our almost exclusive footage of his attack. My mind went back to 1985, when Madiot had won Paris–Roubaix with an identical attack in exactly

At last! Gilbert Duclos-Lasalle came home as victor in 1992, winning at his fourteenth attempt

The prize: Jean-Marie Wampers had just enough strength left to hold his winner's cobblestone aloft in 1989

the same place. I thought too of the circumstances that may have helped his escape that year: Garcia's motorbike had turned over in the slippery mud at the very moment Madiot made his move, completely blocking the narrow track from behind!

Today the conditions were too dry for similar accidents, but the recollection inspired me to make a quick calculation as to when we'd last seen a 'real' Hell of the North. Six years it had been – more than half a decade since that memorable edition of the race when so many stirring images were recorded. Because of the comparative dryness of following years, the muddy memories of 1985 have remained clear in my mind ever since, and will continue to do so should this drought continue in the years to come.

Madiot was going like a train now on this penultimate section of cobbles and I drew Luke back for some more of the action, more relaxed now that the race had taken a definitive turn at last. I used a 135mm lens to get a close-up of Madiot's contorted face, but knew that the pounding of the cobbles would limit the number of usable frames, as the vibrations worked their way up through the bike's wheels and suspension into my hands. It was no mean fluke that the best images to come out of this attack were taken by *L'Equipe's* Denys Clement aboard Garcia's bike. Apart from Garcia's enviable reputation, Clement's hefty bulk apparently absorbs the vibrations better than the sleeker bodies of most of his colleagues – an 'asset' he seemed particularly proud of when explaining the secrets of his success a week later.

For the most part, photographers are obliged to leave for the finish of a big race before the last five kilometres; but the peculiarity of this race, finishing as it does on a velodrome, means it is best to give oneself a few extra minutes. So it was that we accelerated away with eight kilometres left, leaving just a few daring photographers near to the action.

The approach to Roubaix is made through a maze of tiny, narrow streets, with left and right turns coming at you with incessant regularity, and with a most unphotogenic backdrop of grimy industrial buildings; we were missing nothing by leaving the race so soon. Then, with just a few kilometres left, the route swings right into a tree-lined avenue, where thousands of Roubaix citizens now waited outside their homes to cheer Madiot home, having probably seen his escape live on their TV screens. The entrance to the track is found via a sinuous route away from the avenue, and all motorised transport is stopped at the track opening itself. I jumped down from Luke's bike, slapping him cheerily on the back, then ran into the track centre and across to the enclosure set aside for us. The stadium was alive with emotion, the French fans overwhelmed by Madiot's escape.

That emotion spilled over as Madiot made his entry into the velodrome – a dot of white dwarfed by the large stadium and by the colourful mass cheering his every move around the shallow, grey banking. I focused in on the day's hero as he crossed the finish line with one lap of the track to cover, his tongue still poked out after 16 kilometres of hard effort. And when he came around again, this time with his hands held high, the hero had come home – home to a welcome fit for a king. Marc Madiot had won his second Paris–Roubaix in six years.

The aftermath of a Paris–Roubaix can be as exciting an event as the actual race, with riders flopping down in the grassy centre, their faces caked with the grime of their trade. Like coalminers emerging from a seven-hour shift, their expressions are sought by cameramen and journalists alike, eager to record any emotion that might give a clue as to that person's particular day in hell, while every few minutes another lone cyclist enters the stadium to rousing cheers – for Paris–Roubaix is as much about the brave finishers as it is about the heroic winners.

ROLF SÖRENSEN

14 OCTOBER 1990: PARIS–TOURS

Four cyclists pounded along the wide highway, tucked down low to dodge the teasing sidewind that nagged at their efforts to stay clear. They were within 15 kilometres of the finish of the Paris–Tours – the 'sprinters' classic' – but the intensity of their efforts dictated another line of thought for these attackers, for they had no intention of handing the race over to the fast finishers. The four – Rolf Sörensen, Phil Anderson, Andreas Kappes and Kim Andersen – were being chased hard by the might of the entire peloton. It was a daunting task this, racing flat-out at over 60 kilometres per hour to stay clear of a Panasonic-led peloton that was sometimes accelerating to 65 kilometres per hour. The four stuck to their chosen self-torture, relaying one another with steady pulls at the front before a short-lived rest in the buffeting slipstream allowed each of them to draw vital breath. It was an impressive sight, these equally talented men riding at their limit to reach Tours ahead of the bunch, and then ahead of each other. I was inspired by their audacity, and moved in as much as possible to record their athleticism.

There was Anderson, his emotions completely masked by the dark Oakley glasses he was wearing. There was Kappes, his dark smouldering determination emphasized by his outsized white headband restraining a mop of long dark hair. There was Andersen, the weakest of the quartet, having ridden hard in a break all day. And there was Sörensen, the ginger-haired Dane with his boy-next-door looks. I stared at his face the most through my 135mm lens, with a growing belief that this was a rider of the future, so quickly was the cyclist maturing. Just ten kilometres left now, and the peloton could be seen two undulations back on this long drag towards Tours.

We quit the race with just five kilometres to go, screaming flat-out to the finish to give ourselves as much time as possible to prepare. Would it be a bunch sprint after all? The chasers were barely 20 seconds behind when I'd last looked, massing powerfully on the empty road behind. We drove onto the long, long finishing straight in Tours – drove seemingly for ever down the tree-lined Avenue de Grammont, graphically aware of how long the chasers would have the escapers in their sights here. Our motorbikes dismissed, we took our positions and waited.

The race approached, preceded by a stampede of late-arriving official cars. From somewhere amongst this a cyclist could be seen, indistinguishable under the shady trees. In a confused instant it was all over; Sörensen flashed across the line just inches ahead of . . . Maurizio Fondriest! Where had he come from? I didn't care just then: I'd been carefully aiming my 180mm lens on Sörensen, not on this late-arrival from Italy; for the Dane had won – won his first big one-day race. Just seconds later the road filled with a swarm of gasping cyclists. Sörensen had held on the longest from his breakaway group – held on by just four seconds from the bunch – a grand finale if ever there was one.

ALFONS DE WOLF

2 MARCH 1983: OMLOOP HET VOLK

We were well into the last third of the race – a 220-kilometre circuit around western Flanders – when the Volkegemstraat suddenly loomed up in front of us. Nearly three kilometres long, and just a few minutes after the Eikenberg, its impact on the race had seemed inevitable from the moment the race had left Ghent that morning. In anticipation, we stopped near the end of the track, at a point where I felt we would see the true story of the Omloop Het Volk unfold.

The sun was as bright as it could possibly be in Belgium on the first Saturday of March, and its clarity emphasised the strength of the colourful mass juddering towards me as I focused through a 180mm lens. Too late to change lenses, I cursed as the motorbike from Belgium's Flemish television station hovered ahead of the race, obscuring my view of whoever was making the running. I kept my sights fixed on the obscure figures dancing in the slipstream of the motorbike as it bounded across my sights. At the last possible instant before the shot was completely lost, the bike passed through my viewfinder, a split second before two powerful figures triggered off my senses to release the shutter.

It was a fleeting snap – so brief and so late that I wasn't even sure I'd got it – and only later did I realise my good fortune in having caught the exact moment Jan Raas and Alfons De Wolf had made their winning escape. I stayed at that spot long enough to capture some images of the reaction to their fierce attack, but really only wanted to get up ahead to see these two in action, so exquisite had their panache been as they'd sped by. Five kilometres later we were there alongside them, watching admiringly as Raas relayed his younger companion with a zest so full of intent, while De Wolf too seemed to thrive on his luck at having secured such an experienced ally.

With 40 kilometres still to go, there was every reason to fear for these riders' destiny, with so many good riders and teams chasing hard. But the two leaders seemed oblivious to the pursuit coming from behind, powering along with scarcely a glance at one another, only thinking

of the racing still to come. They passed through 185 kilometres with 35 seconds in hand, then through 192 kilometres with almost a minute; just 22 kilometres remained. Behind, the chase was at its height, with the teams of Splendor, Aernoudt and Europ-Decor uniting in their efforts to bring Raas back in particular; no Belgian teams wanted a Dutchman to win here. The teams of De Wolf's Bianchi and Raas's indomitable Raleigh were doing their level best to stem the flowing tide, quite literally fighting to protect their leaders' interests up ahead.

Raas and De Wolf were more than up to this counter-challenge, and proved it by moving a further minute ahead as they met the outskirts of Ghent. Onto the impressive Ghentbrugge, and De Wolf tried a sudden attack, but only succeeded in drawing a stinging response from Raas; it seemed likely their private duel would end in a two-up sprint. De Wolf led Raas through the finish line in Zwijnaarde with a small five-kilometre circuit to complete, their much-cheered passage across the town followed more than two minutes later by the Raleigh-suppressed peloton, which bounded nonchalantly across the line in acceptance of defeat. In the sprint it was De Wolf who came in first, scoring his second consecutive win in the Omloop.

The peloton heads towards Bastogne in 1987

LIÈGE-BASTOGNE-LIÈGE

The scene outside the little teashop must have resembled any other Sunday morning in La Roche, a pretty greystone town straddling the banks of the River Ourthe, deep in the beautiful Belgian Ardennes. Tourists, well wrapped up against the cold, wandered about the narrow streets, gazing into antique shop windows or buying a Sunday newspaper before slipping into a warm café for their mid-morning intake of coffee and cake. In the café *Chez Marianne* the majority of clientele was far removed from the normal run-of-the-mill tourist – the batch of motorbikes parked outside indicated that much. Inside the café, the orders were more often for beer or cognac than they were for coffee or tea. And instead of cake, omelette and chips was the favoured menu for the men grouped around a couple of tables.

This third Sunday in April had dawned bright but freezing in the city of Liège, 65 kilometres to the north, and these men – part of the photographers' entourage of the 77th Liège-Bastogne- Liège cycle race – were trying to thaw out from the one-hour drive south, having left the still-sleeping race within half an hour of its departure from Liège. The leaded windows of the café were steamed over with condensation, the heat inside contrasting sharply with the cold outside. When the race had left Liège, the thermometers had shown just two degrees above freezing, and even now, in the wooded valleys of the Ardennes, the level had only crept up to 6 degrees Celsius, with a bleak forecast of snow on offer for the remainder of the day. I wrapped my numb fingers around the mug of hot chocolate in my hands, tingling already with the warmth that the cognac-laced drink sent into my stomach and chest. I hated the thought of snow.

Our presence in the café inspired an excited exchange of conversation between the locals and us, with each and everyone there recalling previous years when *La Doyenne* had encountered snow. I had missed the most famous year, 1980, when Bernard Hinault had blitzed

the race and its frozen participants with a storming solo escape in the steep hills after the turn-round in Bastogne. Manufacturing an eight-minute advantage by the finish, Hinault had left his indelible mark on Liège-Bastogne-Liège, the oldest one-day classic in the world, and in the vilest conditions the race had ever produced. I gazed through the condensation, wondering if we'd see a repeat of those conditions today, and very much regretting not having been there to see Hinault's epic – for days like that don't come too often in a lifetime.

Liège-Bastogne-Liège has gone through considerable changes in its long existence – not least its recent leasing to the organisers of the Tour de France in 1990, following a catalogue of organisational and financial problems faced by the previous organisers, the Royal Cyclist's Pésant Club Liègeois. It was this club that founded the race way back in 1892, two decades before the Tour of Flanders was created. Because of its earlier position in the season, and the image-gathering asset of its cobbled hills, the Tour of Flanders will always remain the more popular of Belgium's two great classics. But with the power of its present French partner, Liège-Bastogne-Liège is already showing signs of a renaissance.

The race is now more professionally organised, more prize money is up for grabs, and the power and influence of the Société du Tour de France has brought greater world attention to this tough event. The Société has also brought a large slice of its Paris-based staff with it, and now French and French-speaking Belgians work alongside each other both inside and out of the race, creating a strange and unique atmosphere. Unquestionably, the French are now in control of *La Doyenne*, even if courtesy obliges them to give the Belgians a working share. In the race itself, the displacement of Belgium's onerous officials is no great loss to anyone – not least the photographers – and the nightmare experiences of the Tour of Flanders and Belgium's other great races are gladly forgotten in the light of the Tour de France officials' greater professionalism and understanding.

The routing has changed too – much more so in 1991 than in the Tour's first Liège–Bastogne–Liège the previous year – although the removal of some of the most legendary climbs has proved unpopular with the Belgian public. The previous year had seen the absence of the Wall of Stockeu – the very climb on which Hinault had launched his attack in 1980 – and Mont Theux, one of the strategic final climbs. In their place had come two new hills: the Côte de Chambralles and the Côte de Fraiture. Coming immediately after the feared and famous climb of La Redoute, these two ascents inflicted further agony on the field – a factor that puzzled a lot of people when they were then left out of the 1991 route and replaced instead by the Côte de Haussire and Côte de Hézalles.

In just the same way as with the Tour of Flanders, the photography of Liège–Bastogne–Liège is influenced by the nature of the Ardennes climbs, and their strategic sequence in the route dictates our working plan every bit as much as the cobbled *bergs* in the Flemish classic. Different as the Ardennes côtes are, with no cobblestones whatsoever, each climb still has to be considered not just for its material worth, but in the context of the race as a whole. In previous years it took delicate timing to photograph the Wall of Stockeu and still make it ahead of the race to the Côte de la Haute Levée; now the challenge is to capture 'the moment' on La Redoute, but to get quickly away before the race reaches the climbs of Hornay and Les Forges.

We'd chosen the town of La Roche-en-Ardenne, not for its scenic charm, nor for its proliferation of warm

Davis Phinney's crash in 1988

cafés, but for its close proximity to the new Haussire climb – one of the highest points in Belgium and a mere four kilometres down the road. We swept en masse out of the town and up the valley to the start of the climb. It seemed warmer now, but that may have been the generous measures of cognac the café's patron had put into my coffee. Either way, my blood was surging, I sensed the imminent rendezvous with a race we'd last seen more than two hours ago. As we drove to the summit of the tree-lined climb, all of us were surprised by the easy gradient; this wasn't a hill in the greatest tradition of *La Doyenne*, despite its five-kilometre length.

I decided to take a look at the descent: from a shallow start, a sheer drop would take the peloton at breakneck speed down to the main road. I took up a position at that junction, calculating the line the riders would be taking as they battled with the downward plunge and the abrupt right-hand turn onto a rising main road; only the shaded woods would spoil an otherwise dramatic location. Our race radio crackled into life – a sure sign that the race was probably on the climb now. But we still had a ten-minute wait before the lone figure of Thierry Bourguignon was sighted as he plunged down the narrow descent, getting dangerously close to the advance guard of officials' motorbikes and cars. The French cyclist made it safely through the sharp turn, and I relocated myself at a point more likely to catch any subsequent mishap from the chasing peloton.

But I had a further seven-minute wait before the chasers themselves plunged down towards me. Bourguignon had been away for more than 50 kilometres, it seemed, having passed through the turn at Bastogne with an advantage of four minutes. His escape had led nicely to the steady chase now being started on the descent of the Côte de Haussire, which in turn had created the gap now visible in the descending group as it cascaded towards the dangerous corner. I waited, I focused – but nobody fell. We drove off after the speeding riders, who had somehow survived intact from the descent and formed an almost complete

peloton again.

As we drove past on the approaches to Houffalize, I couldn't fail to see the grey storm clouds gathering on the horizon – the sunshine that had given me hope in La Roche had suddenly gone, replaced by the imminent threat of snow. I grew cold as we drew closer to the lone figure of Bourguignon, and realised my hands had turned numb as I fumbled with the controls of my camera. It wasn't a good day to have forgotten my gloves. My second picture sequence of this fleeing cyclist, a few minutes later on the summit of the Côte du Bois aux Moines, contained the first snowflakes of what I hated to admit was starting to look like a bad day. I looked on enviously as a French photographer next to me took a swig of something obviously warm from his hipflask, carefully ignoring my looks like a well-practised Parisian waiter.

We were less than 20 kilometres from the Côte de Wanne. Bourguignon began the climb with his lead now down to just three minutes – a drastic reduction brought about by the cold, which had drained his strength while at the same time forcing the peloton to ride faster to keep warm. I'd been caught out by the chasers, having stopped to make running repairs to a camera, and the main group swept by as I ran for the bike. I was obliged to follow the massive group up the spectacular climb, listening angrily as the radio told of Criquielion's accelerations and Argentin's reactions. It took us most of the kilometres separating the summit of the Wanne from the foot of the Hézalles to get around the group, and I made a hasty stop on the lower slopes of this new hill, believing I'd found the best place.

Bourguignon was caught right before my very eyes, firstly by Criquielion's team-mates, then by the entire group, which set about this steep climb with incredible ferocity. The sun had miraculously come out, and I warmed at the sight of the blue skies now materialising above. The group was still 150 strong, and it took a few minutes before we could regain the road behind the last riders. It was only then that I realised I'd missed the

A remnant from the second world war, this American tank marks the turning point in Bastogne, from where a different battle is about to be fought in 1988

our way through, especially as the entire photographic corps was doing the same thing. But we succeeded a few kilometres before the town, and I glanced to my right as we sped past the old right turn that indicated the foot of the famous Wall of Stockeu. The Haute Levée is well placed for spectator access, and they lined the three-kilometre climb four or five deep in places, making our lives difficult when searching for a place to pull in.

I chose a spot well up the climb, where I could see if there was anything worth taking before we committed ourselves to the challenge. I knew a 40-man group was now ahead, and my radio informed me further that Criquielion was on the front. I anticipated the advantages to be had by stopping at an interesting bend just before the summit, and I directed the driver there instead; I'd taken a superb shot of Criquielion on this same bend in the 1985 Liège–Bastogne–Liège, and the face of the man that now filled my viewfinder again seemed hardly to have changed. Only his jersey was different: the black, yellow and red champion-of-Belgium colours instead of the rainbow-chested colours of the world champion.

Criquielion was alone in my shot, having just attacked out of the group, and behind him came a handful of riders – the only men strong enough to match the Belgian's speed. Now back on the bike, I could see that an elite group was forming on the *faux-plat* following the official summit, with Criquielion keeping his momentum at the front, but tracked ever so easily by Moreno Argentin. Behind these two, individuals struggled to make the selection, with Stephen Roche closest to the two forcers, followed inches away by Rolf Sörensen and Johan Bruyneel. I grew excited at seeing Roche riding with champions again, and was equally excited by the sight of Miguel Indurain towing fellow Spaniards Marino Lejarreta and Iñaki Gaston a few metres further back. Raul Alcalá and Eric Van Lancker completed this star-studded selection, which came together only when Criquielion eased up over the actual summit, no doubt content with his work so far.

best part of the climb as the tail-enders turned right into a sharp bend, now forced out of their saddles by a sheer gradient that was far in excess of anything I'd seen before in this race. Thousands of people had gathered on this corner, perched on stone walls or squatting on the grass verges. The noise was deafening as we ourselves took the sharp turn, my driver's heavy Honda bike barely making it, so slowly were we travelling.

Just as after the previous climb, we barely managed to get around the race before it swept into the town of Stavelot and up towards the Côte de la Haute Levée. The last hill had smashed the race into three or four pieces, and it took tender care on the part of my driver to work

The race had come to life dramatically on the Haute Levée, and I wondered if it was already over, so devastating had Criquielion's attack been. Now behind the breakaways, we swept down the long, long descent towards Francorchamps and Spa, passing right over the start line of the previous Wednesday's Flèche Wallonne, which Argentin had won in such magnificent style. After the town I took the opportunity to get ahead for the Côte de Rosier and a few seconds' respite. The race was shaping up nicely; the threat of snow had long since been forgotten as the hills had cast their magic on the race – and, so far at least, the French officials had been kind to our commercial needs in the race. The Rosier climb is tranquil compared to its precedents in the race, with virtually no spectators whatsoever – only the attractiveness of its surroundings on a wide plateau amid the lush green hillsides.

Next came the Côte de Lorcé: a climb first introduced the previous year, although not exceptionally difficult – merely an appetiser, in fact, for La Redoute. The leaders were convincingly ahead already, their nearest challengers being an RMO-led chase two minutes behind, with just over 40 kilometres remaining. As I waited at the roadside above the hamlet of Targnon, I smiled at our change in fortune at the hands of the weather. Whereas grey skies and snow flurries had seemed to be our fate just one hour before, now there was just blue sky with puffy white clouds to illuminate our day in the Ardennes. The sun shone directly into the leaders' faces as they rode, creating a perfect composition in my Nikon's viewfinder.

I knew I was getting my best shots in the race now, and lingered long enough in front of the riders to the point where an official gave me a warning over the radio. So I decided it would be a good idea to take a look at the chasing group, still two minutes back, as there wouldn't be another chance after La Redoute. The group of 35 riders was still led by the RMO team, whose star rider Charly Mottet had missed the move on Haute Levée. They were helped occasionally by the Buckler team, no doubt hoping that Edwig Van Hooydonck could jump across to the leaders if the gap was brought down.

However, sensing I was watching a losing battle, I asked my driver to get back to the leaders, and go on to La Redoute, as quickly as possible; we passed the Argentin-led group in Aywaille with just 35 kilometres remaining. It had been more than six hours since we'd passed through the same town that morning, only now we were going in the opposite direction with about an hour's racing – and three hills – remaining. It promised to be an exciting finale.

We sped on towards Remouchamps – a town whose narrow, twisty streets directed the race on towards La Redoute, the most spectacular ascent in the whole race. Since a near-catastrophe on the climb in 1985, when a combination of too many motorbikes and vociferous spectators caused one cyclist to fall, all press cars are now diverted around the hill, and photographers have to take a strange diversion halfway up the climb to thwart any ambitions they may have of working from their motorbikes on this sheer ascent.

The narrow track eventually brought us to the top of the climb, where we were obliged to find the best spot amongst the excited spectators, fighting with some of the drunker ones who resented us crouching in front. Even though we had been speeding ahead of the race for more than 15 kilometres, taking the diversion meant that only a few minutes remained before the leaders arrived. In fact, spectators' radios told us that Sörensen had attacked in the town below. From our position it was possible to look down onto the motorway that passes above the bottom of the climb, and I could just distinguish a line of cars that had pulled off the speed track, their passengers clapping Sörensen's progress as he began the climb.

Soon the wall of spectators swayed and jostled down the climb, agitated by the arrival of a television motorbike, which skilfully filmed the Dane's climb as he came into view. The white-jerseyed rider streaked through my camera sights, just inches behind the

Claude Criquielion tried in vain to win Liège-Bastogne-Liège just once during his career, but without success. Here this popular rider leads a breakaway group up the Côte de Lorcé in 1991

motorbike filming his every move, and precise reactions were needed to get any sort of shot. Thirty seconds later the second TV motorbike raced into view, and this time the spectators went wild, for the champion of Belgium was leading now – leading his rivals a dance up the steep ascent, yet all the while dogged by Argentin's attentions. This time the motorbike blocked my view of the two attackers, and instead I had to settle for a grabbed shot of Indurain as the tall Spaniard sprinted across the widening gap. Fifteen seconds later came four more riders: Roche and Lejarreta, trailed by Alcalá and Van Lancker. There was no sign of Bruyneel or Gaston now.

I waited longer still, looking for Phil Anderson, but ran back to the bike after photographing Eric Breukink – it was dangerous to wait any longer, I knew. We sped off after the dropped riders, squeezing past them on the tiny lanes after the summit of La Redoute. But already I realised I'd overstayed my welcome on the hill, for it would take quite a while to work past so many riders. In the time it had taken me to get back onto the motorbike, about 20 riders had gone past. Eventually we arrived on the wide main road near Sprimont, and quickly accelerated past all the chasers and up to Roche's group. Also with us was Jean-Marie Leblanc in his red Fiat car. Clearly nervous of allowing us by, he ordered us to stay where we were, and I could understand his anxiety; the leaders were tantalisingly close, just 200 metres in front.

After Sprimont came the main-road climb of Hornay, and from where I stood I could see everything up ahead, so close was Roche's group to that of Criquielion. I was so close myself that I could recognise each of the photographers as they worked in front of the leaders – a sight that made me impatient and frustrated, as I was missing the most important moves in the race. I looked appealingly at Leblanc, then indicated with my hand I wanted to get past: 'Non!' he shouted 'It's too risky now.' I looked at my colleagues behind me: they too were beginning to panic, not least my good friend Piet Van Belle, who worked for Belgium's biggest newspaper *Het*

Miguel Indurain raced hard up the Côte de Chambralles in 1990

In 1987, Stephen Roche rode hard up the climb of Hornay just ahead of Moreno Argentin, and will soon leave the Italian world champion behind in an effort to win the race

The Côte des Forges saw a desperate chase by Laurent Fignon and Sean Kelly in 1985, up ahead Moreno Argentin, Claude Criquielion and Stephen Roche pull clear

*Robert Millar finished third in 1988, having done more than his
fair share of the work. He's seen here on the Côte de Hornay,
leading eventual winner Adrie Van Der Poel*

Nieuwsblad. He'd be shot by his editor if he didn't bring
home the goods.

The leaders seemed to be pulling away again as we
cleared the town, and again I caught Leblanc's attention:
surely he could let us go past, one by one? He shrugged
apologetically; still the answer was 'Non!' I became
annoyed. All any of us wanted to do was to get ahead of
the leaders, fearful of missing pictures of this all-
important segment of the race. Leblanc clearly didn't

trust some of us to do just that, no doubt suspecting that
one of us would hesitate in front of the chasers for a
quick shot and perhaps aid their acceleration. What it
felt to be convicted without trial! Every year the race
explodes on La Redoute, and every year the same
situation occurs on the run-in to Liège, with the gap
between leaders and chasers never greater than half a
minute – and usually a lot less. I suspected that Leblanc,
who had only one year's experience of directing *La*

Doyenne, was following Belgian officials' advice to the letter on this particular problem – and we were suffering for it!

All that remained was the climb of the Côte des Forges, eight kilometres away, then the 14-kilometre drop into Liège itself. I prayed Leblanc would let us past before Les Forges, and maintained my place at the front of the long line of motorbikes immediately behind Leblanc's car, hoping to be the first to go through. The gap between the four riders directly ahead of us and the four men just a few hundred metres in front was now timed at 15 seconds by the mobile timekeepers – aboard motorbikes that had the complete freedom of the road. I could see Leblanc's point of view still, as the leaders were very close, but I knew that individually we could

all get past without interfering with the race. However, I had no means of explaining that to him amidst the cacophony of noise all around us.

We were now descending towards the start of the Côte des Forges, and as we swung onto the wide climb, I noticed the leaders were just pulling out of sight around a bend a hundred metres ahead. Despite the mounting pressure on him, Leblanc kept his composure as I made a successful request to go right up to the leaders. Promising not to film the chasers, we squeezed past Roche's right shoulder to accelerate to the front of the race. The gap was perhaps just 150 metres, and we were soon ahead of Sörensen, who was controlling the leaders' movements in the interests of his team-mate Argentin. It had been more than 13 kilometres since we'd last seen the front of the race – a massive 20 minutes' redundancy at the most crucial part of the day. To compound my exasperation, we were now riding in the shadows of the trees overhanging Les Forges, having missed the lower two-thirds of this final climb. I could do nothing more than pull away to the top of the hill, hoping for a patch of sunlight to satisfy my unproductive camera skills.

The previous year, Van Lancker had attacked on this final climb, and I'd got an unusual shot of him from behind as he'd crested the summit, filmed by two photographers who, like me, had been surprised at the ease with which we'd been allowed to record the Belgian's escape. In previous years I'd achieved similar successes on Les Forges, none more so than when Steven Rooks had attacked way back in 1983. But those happy-go-lucky days are behind us now, eclipsed by ever more stifling regulations that have made our work so hard. This year, the officials were very agitated by the problem of having so many angry photographers to contend with, and only a few of us ventured near the leaders as Indurain blazed a path through the massive crowds filling the wide highway at the summit of the Côte des Forges.

Our radio reported the gap to be still in the region of

Moreno Argentin easily won his fourth Liège–Bastogne–Liège in
1991, outsprinting the ever hopeful Claude Criquielion

Three steps to victory: Stephen Rooks senses his companions, Stephen Roche and Jostein Willmann are in trouble on the Côte des Forges; he pressures them with this attack; pulls away with ease – suitably witnessed by photographers

just 20 seconds as we began the long, steady descent towards Liège. If I'd entertained any thoughts of being allowed lengthy stays at the sides of the leaders because of my delayed arrival from behind the chasers, I was wrong. Between Les Forges and the final kilometres in Liège, I got near them twice, but only with long lenses, and on each occasion facing the close scrutiny and wrath of the race's chief 'regulator' – one of two such officials responsible for regulating the photographers' motorbikes ahead of the race. Theirs is an intimidating presence, reinforced by the knowledge that you'll be needing their favours in another race – in this French official's case, the Tour de France in July. Usually the Société du Tour's officers are respectful of our editorial needs; but today the presence of so many motorbikes at such a delicately balanced point in the race had clearly pushed these officials' humour too far.

On both occasions when I had got near, Criquielion had been doing all the forcing, clearly trying to win Liège–Bastogne–Liège before his impending retirement. And each time I'd taken those few precious frames, it had always been with half an eye on the chasers, who could be seen on the near-horizon. Despite this, I felt the race was as good as over, with two Ariostea riders in the lead group. We quit the race with about five kilometres to go, racing along the Meuse river embankment right towards the centre of Liège, where the finish line had been placed on the Quai Mativa. Last year Van Lancker had come home in style there, as the lone winner of Liège–Bastogne–Liège. But who would win this time? Only a madman would have wagered against Argentin – the Italian seeking his fourth win in this Belgian classic.

We had but a short minute to compose ourselves after the rigours of the last hour; then the four leaders came into view down the wide, wide road. Sörensen seemed to be leading out the sprint, looking across at Criquielion, who had suddenly turned sprinter for his last chance at victory. But within 200 metres of the line, it was the orange jersey of Argentin that came to the

The feared slopes of La Redoute did not stop Dirk de Wolf from riding to a brilliant victory in 1992. The Flemish cyclist is leading Stephen Rooks on the 20 percent gradient

fore, making the others seem pedestrian in his wake. The Venetian threw his arms high as he approached the line – a gesture matched by team-mate Sörensen, who had retained first place in the World Cup competition.

Another Belgian classic was over, another dose of life with the hard men finished. Liège–Bastogne–Liège will always be rated as one of the toughest classics of all – its menu of Ardenne climbs ever variable but always decisive; its fickle weather always ready to crucify all but the strongest men. But *La Doyenne* will never be my favourite race: its intemperate disintegration at each passing hill may be full of suspense, but so soon after the cobbled classics of Flanders, Ghent–Wevelgem and Paris–Roubaix, even its explosive finale seems impotent. It will be nearly a whole year before the classics return once again to Belgium – to the land that brought a whole new meaning to the word 'classic'.

CHARLY MOTTET

15 OCTOBER 1988: TOUR OF LOMBARDY

The little figure in front of us was all so familiar, his neat, compact body tucked stylishly low over the bike as he plummeted down the twisty descent of the Col di Valpiana, still 70 kilometres away from the finish in Milan. Charly Mottet's winning ambitions had been nicely set up on the vicious 20-kilometre-long Valico di Valcava a short while earlier, where the Frenchman had at one stage had the company of Marino Lejarreta, Luc Roosen and Claude Criquielion with him. Showing his determination Mottet had left his companions on the summit itself, descending crazily into the valley lest anyone should chance joining up with him later.

On the summit of the Valpiana, Mottet had taken time to change to a lighter bike in preparation for the long, flat highway into the industrial capital of Italy, and it was this machine that he was so skilfully employing now as he raced dangerously at 80 kilometres per hour through the leafy corners and straights. For those of us following it was an impressive sight – one made all the more memorable when it became clear how much Mottet himself was enjoying this spectacle. Only at one particularly sharp bend, where he had to brake hard following too fast an approach, did the Frenchman falter, and even then he had the audacity to look back at all of us, a self-mocking grin creeping across his face.

Only two motorbikes had managed to stay with Mottet by the time he'd arrived on the sprawling main road, and both drivers were quickly alongside him, giving us a first chance to photograph this amazing escape, while they – Patrice and Jacques Garcia – both took the time to shout their respects to Mottet for his near-perfect descent. Mottet had attained a fine advantage of one minute and 40 seconds as he'd begun the long run home – a lead that quickly crept beyond two minutes as his bulbous calf muscles switched into pursuit mode. With 40 kilometres still to go, Mottet was maintaining his lead despite the build-up of chasers behind, with Gianni Bugno and Lejarreta the most dangerous, having now detached themselves from a larger group after the descent.

Up ahead, Mottet kept driving along, his small physique belying his body's strengths and the strength of mind being used to achieve his goal. His legs worked like well-oiled pistons as they pumped the pedals hard, only the bulging muscles providing any hint as to the effort his body was making, while his photogenic face hung open in true time-trialling fashion. I'd seen him in this superb form just one week earlier in the Grand Prix des Nations time trial, where he'd broken the course record en route to winning his third title in the French race; and it was the same mastery now being so finely displayed in Italy. Approaching Milan, his chasers Bugno and Lejarreta had drawn close, but never close enough to endanger his magnificent achievement. Mottet cruised down the Corso Buenos Aires still 1:40 ahead to win his first-ever one-day classic race.

PHIL ANDERSON

24 APRIL 1983: AMSTEL GOLD

They could be seen closing in from behind – a group of perhaps 20 men on this highway to Maastricht, closing in on the five-man breakaway group that had escaped on the ascent of the Keuternberg. It was on this climb, by far the hardest in the race, that Phil Anderson made his move, forcing his muscular body up the hill to draw Joop Zoetemelk, Jan Raas, Michel Pollentier and Ludo Peeters away, with Pascal Simon joining on the descent. But they were always in sight of the chasers, who included Adrie Van der Poel and Gerrie Knetteman, two of Holland's most famous classic specialists, as well as Sean Kelly, Gregor Braun and Etienne de Wilde. It wasn't therefore surprising that we now saw Anderson's attempt at victory under threat.

But he thought otherwise, and suddenly sprinted away to keep the initiative. Zoetemelk went with him and the two stepped up their offensive with renewed vigour, whilst behind them their one-time allies in the break looked to Raas to make a move. Anderson and Zoetemelk piled on the pressure, relaying each other with flat-out commitment and strength to push their advantage beyond the reach of their pursuers. Being Dutch, Zoetemelk's potential chasers were few indeed, and even then, very tentative when it came to making the running. The two leaders gave their all, now on the road to Valkenburg, and arrived in the town centre 40 seconds to the good. Just the Cauberg remained.

No sooner had they begun this final climb than Anderson launched his attack, soaring up into the crowd-blocked road like a madman running amok in a crowded bazaar. The crowds parted at the last second, their absence creating an uncertain path up the hill, and Anderson bounded along, his heavy upper body hanging over the handlebars in raw style, while his famous teeth flashed as he gasped for breath at the height of his acceleration. The Australian cleared the hill with 50 metres in hand, and began the final 15-kilometre run-in to the finish in Meerssen in the knowledge that Zoetemelk wouldn't give up easily – certainly not in Holland. Anderson rode like a crazed one, tucked low over his handlebars to decrease wind resistance, his face fixed.

It was a sight I'd waited two years to see, realising the Australian's world-class potential in the summer of 1981 on the Tour de France stage to Pla d'Adet in the Pyrenees, when he'd outclimbed Bernard Hinault to the finish that day, and pitched himself in to win the Yellow Jersey. The determination of the man I photographed today was no different, only his experience was greater, and I grew excited at Anderson's fierce profile as we drove alongside him on the dropping highway. Just eight kilometres remained now: even with just 30 seconds to spare, I felt he had it in the bag. I quit for the finish in the outskirts of Meerssen, convinced I'd taken the best shots of that spring's classics, and smilingly took my place amongst the other photographers packed into the finish area. The victorious Anderson followed home a short while later, his victory salute so genuine in the light of his first-ever classic win. It had been a great day.

TOUR OF LOMBARDY

The view from the roadway made me gasp, made me want to shriek with joy. I was standing on a sweeping bend of the Passo Intelvi, high above Lake Como on a warm October afternoon. It had been a beautiful day, all day, there in the northern lake region of Italy, where nature created the perfect weld between flatland and mountain, between material creations and those more godly – and where for the past 74 years the Giro di Lombardia – in English, Tour of Lombardy – has brought the professional racing season to a close amidst a most poignant setting. I became enchanted with this race on that fateful day in 1982, when my efforts in driving more than 1,000 miles from London were more than justified by the sight alone of the deep blue lake spread out before my eyes, from whose shores the colourful peloton was about to climb directly towards me.

It had seemed mad at the time, taking off for Italy on the spur of the moment. It was as if I was trying to salvage one last dreg of satisfaction from the season – trying to make it last that little bit longer, as if afraid a new season might never come around, or if it did that it might not be quite so compelling. My feelings have changed very little since then – in fact they've probably strengthened – and every year I make the journey to Italy with the same conviction that this is the one race to be enjoyed above all, lest anything should one day stop me from photographing the Tour of Lombardy.

21 OCTOBER 1991: FIERA DI MONZA

Those still blue waters of Lake Como had seemed a million miles away when I'd collected my accreditation from Signor Flavio Astori late the previous afternoon, and our arrival this morning at the same location had brought with it little cause for optimism; the place was a depressing dump. The prefabricated building that served as the race headquarters was set in an area of

The peloton climbs away from Lake Como in 1985

urban wasteland on the edge of Monza, just across from the city's football stadium, and only a few tantalising kilometres from the grandeur of the city centre, which itself lies only a short distance from Milan. I couldn't understand how the organisers had allowed themselves to devalue the race's romantic aura in such a way, when it would have been so much more appropriate to have started from the historic centre, with its cobbled streets and impressive domed churches.

I busied myself around Patrice's motorbike, silently cursing the circumstances that had threatened my affection for the race. The weather wasn't helping either, for dawn had brought dull, overcast skies, which I knew would deprive me of capturing any of those wondrous lakeside panoramas I'd so enthused over in 1982. The Giro di Lombardia is as much about the lakes of northern Italy as it is about its competitive importance as the final classic of the season. And every year since its inception in 1905, the 'race of the falling leaves' has rekindled the dying embers of a season in a way that now draws a melancholy veil over my eyes. Because of its late slot in the cycling calendar, and the consequent lethargy on the part of top riders in recent years, it is the autumnal colouring of the Lombardian vegetation that has tweaked that last piece of romanticism in me in a way that no other race can even approach.

In the years since that first sight of the Giro di Lombardia, the routing of the race has changed drastically, but it has always, always, retained its close proximity to the lakes. In the past the Giro di Lombardia started in Milan and took the race on a spectacular approach into the hills above Lecco, before skirting the eastern shore of Lake Como. It then ran along the opposite shore in the second half of the race, taking in half a dozen climbs on its run-in to the finish in Como.

The alternative route introduced in 1986 was no less spectacular: Como and Milan swapped places as starting and finishing points, but most importantly the lakeside tours continued. However, instead of using climbs such as the Passo Intelvi, Monte di Argegno and San Fermo

*Claude Criquielion, Bernard Hinault and Pedro Delgado climb
the Colle di Balisio in 1984*

della Battaglia, the race went up into the eastern hills, onto the Valico di Esino Lario, the Valico di Valcava and the Colle di Valpiana. The most famous climb in the Giro di Lombardia's history is the Madonna del Ghisallo, made legendary by the deeds of Fausto Coppi during the 1940s, when many of the roads around Lake Como were unpaved – an experience far removed from today's smoother surfaces. In some years this climb is used on the return leg to the finish, while in other years it comes as an *hors d'oeuvre*. The ascent from the Lecco side of the lake is the most feared, with umpteen hairpin bends which, although not cobbled like the Passo Intelvi, nevertheless create an unsteadily increasing gradient as the climb progresses.

It was on the slopes of this climb in 1985 that Sean Kelly initiated the move that was to win him his second Lombardy race, and I can still remember to this day the Irishman's attack on the steepest section that dislodged all but three of the riders that year. I now wondered whether the Ghisallo ascent today would be as rewarding for Kelly, for it came within 50 kilometres of the finish, and was to be followed by the sharp climbs of the Colle de Brianza and the Lissolo. It seemed the perfect battleground for a Kelly 'special'.

In accordance with its innocuous starting point, the 74th Giro inched its way out of the makeshift car park by the back exit – a sight so imponderable it seemed better to close one's eyes until it was all over. The race

The peloton descends past the memorial chapel at the summit of the Madonna del Ghisallo in 1984

did a slow, congested circuit of the headquarters before lining up again for its official start in the main road alongside. I cringed at the thought that in approximately seven hours we'd once again have to contend with the prevailing ambience of the Fiera di Monza, for the race would finish in exactly the same place as where we now waited, listening for the starter's signal so we could make our move. The former starting places in Milan, and especially Como, with its luxurious lakeside piazza, seemed to belong to another race altogether. Thankfully the pace went wild, immediately accelerating up to 60 kilometres per hour on the wide road to Trezzo sull' Adda, from where the race would make its turn towards the lakes. I wondered if the cyclists weren't merely fleeing the insulting start location to regain their dignity.

Despite its romanticism only the most serious of photographers make the trip to Lombardy, hanging on to the tail-end of the season in the hope that one famous rider or another will add his own particular notoriety to the race – and make their visit all the more worthwhile. Then there are the photographers like me who would come here anyway, regardless of the materialistic attractions, of which, today, there seemed to be few indeed. Even the new world champion Gianni Bugno had given the race a miss, despite the fact that it started in his home town. In spite of all this, I was optimistic that the day augured well for me, and I got stuck in at the first opportunity, firing off a few frames of Maurizio Fondriest, the leader of the world cup competition, as he shed some of his jerseys alongside the Panasonic team car.

It seemed one of the small attacks was making some headway along the road, but I ignored this distraction for now, preferring to overtake everything and stop at a nice café along the lake. It was so cold. By the time two breakaways had passed the café, on the outskirts of Lecco, we'd been joined by the other photographers in the race, all of us sharing a last snack together before the season drew to a close; we had plenty of time to swap stories on our season, and thoughts on the coming

Robert Millar stormed up the hard side of the Madonna del Ghisallo in 1985 ahead of eventual race-winner – Sean Kelly

Autumnal light illuminates this shot of Claude Criquielion leading his friend Sean Kelly on the climb to Esino Lario in 1984

Maurizio Fondriest, the reigning 1988 World Champion, climbs the Valico di Valcava

Gianni Bugno struggles on the Valcava climb in 1990 with Sean Kelly and Eric Caritoux

winter. However, Thierry Gouvenou and Jan Svorada had attained a massive four-minute lead already, with just 60 kilometres covered. Surprised by this, all of us fled the café in pursuit of the leaders, sensing that this was part of a race plan drawn up by the teams of Colnago and 'Z'.

We chased after the pair, catching them about eight kilometres along the eastern side of the lake, shortly before the point where Lake Lecco is absorbed into the larger Lake Como to form a strange lambda-shaped stretch of water. On the horizon was mountain scenery, and I wasted little time in finding a vantage spot on someone's garden wall, quickly sizing up a picture of the peloton riding along the lake with the snow-capped peaks in the background. Despite the overcast conditions, the image seemed to work, and I clambered back down to Patrice's bike, anxious to get ahead of the group before the first climb began, out of Varenna. This year, the race approached the junction to the hill from the south. On previous occasions, at least since 1988,

we'd come from the opposite direction, and in the second half of the race; today the start of the Esino Lario would be reached after just 85 kilometres. And worse still, the organisers had taken out the gruelling ascent of the Valico di Valcava.

The Valcava was introduced in 1986, in a drastic move away from the race's popular use of the Intelvi and Schignano ascents on the western side of Lake Como, which had been put to such good use since the course changes of 1961. The steepness and length of the Valcava changed the 'sporting' image of the Giro di Lombardia, and put the race into the climbers' hands, just one week after the Paris–Tours classic had done a similar thing for the sprinters. Despite the fact that this new routing found universal disfavour with the season-fatigued cyclists – although not the photographers! – Torriani insisted on the Valcava for three more years. Dispensing with the Valcava today had been a big gamble on winning back the true all-rounders, just as in the good old days. I was eager to see how things went.

Sensing the Esino Lario climb might be the only real chance we had to record some agony today, I grew anxious. We had to get ahead, but luck went against us: on the narrow lakeside road there was simply no place to pass, and we swung right onto the climb in last place – last place, that is, in the peloton, for we were the only motorbike crew stupid enough to have got caught behind, and had the road to ourselves at the back. I could see all of my colleagues on the road above us, shooting off dozens of shots of the chasing group, while I cringed down below. My erstwhile confrère Denys Clement teasingly waved to me – he knew how I felt. But he was also Patrice's closest friend, and Clement's gesture incited Patrice to take off suddenly and work his way through the group, ignoring all the rules for such a situation, and despite the inconvenience it was going to cause the riders as they attacked the 16-kilometre climb. Patrice never relented, coolly ignoring the riders' complaints as we cut into their sacred line at each hairpin bend to work our way up the peloton. It was just as well I didn't bother to restrain him!

A few minutes after we'd started from the back, we found ourselves squeezing past Clement himself as he worked away at the front of the big group that was in sight of the 1,000-metre-high summit. Patrice did his level best to block Clement's sights, but the approaching summit persuaded him otherwise; the initial descent was a brute – all loose gravel and hairpin bends. We shot away, out of trouble for now, as the teams of Del Tongo and Toshiba increased the pressure on the main group, which by now had gobbled up both Gouvenou and Svorada.

Ignoring the initial drop, we went on instead to the real plunge – a sinuous plummet down through groves of hawthorn trees, through which the lake could just be glimpsed but not photographed. Stopping once to get a shot from one of the bends as the leading group made their downward swoop, we caught up with them on the descent into Intróbio, from where the race climbed the back of the Colle di Balisio. The latter was a relic of

Viatcheslav Ekimov works hard to bring Fondriest, pedalling hard behind, back to the main group in 1991

earlier Lombardy races that mounted it in the opposite direction – a tougher proposition altogether. This year's gentler climb took us to the drop into Lecco – our second visit there on today's itinerary – before switching northwestwards onto the triangle of land that separates the southern arms of Lakes Como and Lecco. Awaiting us at the tip of this headland should have been the hard side of the Madonna del Ghisallo, but a last-minute problem with roadworks had forced the organisers to abandon this approach, opting instead for a climb of the easier side, followed by what had been credited as a 'super-Ghisallo'!

Thus it was that we passed the Ghisallo summit from the south, trailing a hundred-strong group as it serenely passed the pretty chapel on the right – a chapel known to thousands of bike fans as a permanent shrine to Fausto Coppi. Once, many years ago, I'd ventured in there while awaiting the race, and become spellbound by the jumble of Coppi memorabilia: his bikes, his old Bianchi jerseys, even his pink *Maglia-Rosa* jerseys, lovingly framed for posterity – and all this displayed amid the very sacred atmosphere of a thousand lit candles and ornate statuettes. Today I had no such time, or patience, for I was now in drastic need of reassurance that this Giro di Lombardia was going to live up to the reputation of its predecessors – the 'super-Ghisallo' had better be good! The impromptu ascent began just a kilometre down from the chapel, with a sudden swing left and then a shuddering 15-percent incline.

At first my adrenalin rose inside me, so excited was I that the climb appeared to be as good as its name. But the initial gradient levelled off somewhat, reducing my hopes of a massive explosion within the race to a more modest anticipation of a decisive move. The climb was pretty – one couldn't deny that – but the overhanging trees reduced my hopes even further; I had to make do with shooting landscapes of the race as it meandered through the leafy forests. Then, on one of the last bends of the climb, my viewfinder showed up a sudden attack: Rominger had suddenly accelerated, and all hell had

been let loose behind him.

Excited by this, or perhaps just desperate, Patrice and I dropped back on the next *lacet*, for I wanted to get in close in case the attack came to nothing. We hovered close to the action, but it was another Toshiba rider that came into my sights first. However, I'd spotted an old familiar face in the background: Sean Kelly. We dropped in behind the leader, Martial Gayant, and I aimed my camera and its 135mm lens towards Kelly's face – a face whose expression I'd almost forgotten in such situations. It seemed years since I'd focused so intently on this man's strained features, and it took me a while to compose myself amid the surprise. Yet as I looked into his steely grey-blue eyes, I saw a glint in them that I'd not seen since the 1988 Tour of Spain. My heart jumped at the implications of this, and I completely forgot that Gayant was pulling away.

We dropped to the tail-end of the leading group, which had grown to 50-strong and contained all the major 'names' – Ballerini, Kelly, Fondriest, Alcalá, Rominger, Sörensen – as well as Gayant, who had eased up at the summit. The group swooped down the rapid descent, with us and a couple of other photographers in hot pursuit. Almost halfway down, and a sudden switch in the line of riders caught my eye. At first I thought there'd been a crash, but then I spotted a cluster of red Panasonic jerseys at the side of the road. Fondriest had punctured his front wheel and fallen over in the dirt. Patrice pulled up as soon as he dared, wary of a fast-approaching line of team cars coming up behind us.

Of course Jacques Garcia had stopped right next to Fondriest, affording his photographer, Clement, an exclusive series of pictures as the Panasonic boys swapped Fondriest's bad wheel with one of their own and then pushed him back into the race; their team car had gone straight by, uninformed of their leader's predicament as the race radio remained silent. I sensed something happening now – Fondriest's timing was just too bad to be true. But our radio wasn't working, and I was blissfully unaware that a ten-strong group had

113

Adrie Van der Poel keeps the pace high on the San Fermo di Battaglia in 1983, hoping to weaken Kelly's sprinting legs on this final climb and with a very determined LeMond hard on his heels

attacked at the end of the descent just as Fondriest had been grounded. We raced down, behind the quartet of Panasonic riders, all of them racing flat-out to get back to the main group. Viatcheslav Ekimov was doing the strongest pulls on the front, which in itself was a sight for sore eyes, while Fondriest sat snugly behind, confident that his young Estonian team-mate would get him back.

Without any officials present, I got the best series of pictures so far that day, and had long since put my

cameras aside by the time Fondriest's group rode into the sanctuary of the group up ahead. There was a strange ease with which the group was racing, now just 65 kilometres from home, and we drove up through the group, looking to see what had happened to Kelly's involvement up on the climb. I couldn't see him anywhere, nor for that matter Rolf Sörensen or Franco Ballerini, who'd both been with Kelly on the climb. Slowly it dawned on me that a group of riders had flown, taking advantage, it seemed, of Fondriest's misfortune.

We went to the head of the group, where half the PDM team were now massed. Their controlling the race in this way confirmed my thoughts – that, and the absence of any race cars on the road ahead.

We accelerated clear, eager to get across to whatever breakaway had formed after Fondriest's stoppage. I was surprised how much time the escapers had gained over such a short distance, but when their identities became clear it was no wonder. From Del Tongo there was Ballerini, from Ariostea Sörensen, from Toshiba Gayant, from 'Z' Bruno Cornillet; only Dante Rezze from RMO and Alberto Volpi of Gatorade were surprise participants – and of course there was Kelly, already burying himself at the front in his anxiety to get this break away.

I couldn't wait to get involved too, and Patrice placed me directly in front of the group when Kelly again took his turn, relayed soon after by Sörensen. I was pleased to see the Dane there at this point in the day: his recovery from the crash that had put him out of the Tour de France was nearer completion. Fondriest, the rider who had taken over Sörensen's leadership in the World Cup during the summer, must have been a worried man in the main group, now more than a minute behind – and, I suspected, an angry man, having been left disrespectfully behind in this way. Two climbs remained, the most severe being the Colle de Brianza, which was just a few kilometres away, then shortly after that the smaller ascent of the Lissolo.

Knowing me as well as he does, Patrice only moved me close to the action whenever Kelly rode at the front – which in this particular situation was quite often. I was thrilled at photographing the old man's racing physique once again, because it had been so long since I'd last cherished such moments. As we hovered alongside the Irishman, the memories of him in previous attacks in the Giro di Lombardia came flooding back. Whereas I now focused in on him in his distinct PDM colours, I remembered doing the same in 1983, when his colours had been those of SEM-Mavic, and his escaping

companions had been of the calibre of Greg LeMond, Adrie Van der Poel, Claude Criquielion, Marino Lejarreta and of course Stephen Roche. On that day it had been Roche's patriotic efforts that had helped Kelly to win his first-ever classic victory. What a memorable day that had been!

We were now on the Colle di Brianza, and Kelly was as ever at the front, guiding his companions strongly but cautiously up the severe slopes so as not to lose their assistance later, yet undoubtedly unnerving them with his growing strength and confidence. Still, I felt the Irishman was being overly cautious, for I wanted him to ride into Monza alone, in the style appropriate to his stature. To his side rode Ballerini, a menacing rival if ever there was one. I hoped Kelly had what it takes.

Halfway up the nine-kilometre climb, I decided to take one last look at the chasers, after a radio announcement that they were now over three minutes behind and losing ground all the way. I waited at least a minute longer than that, but then didn't even bother recording the image, as all I could see down the road was a pedestrian-like procession guided by PDM riders. We moved away before the group reached us, and got back up to Kelly just as his group began the descent towards the village of Olgiate.

The roads were narrow now, meandering through forests in full autumnal colouring – a pictorial diversion that went unnoticed by the race official in charge of the breakaway group. The Italian man had already had words with me for apparently staying so close to Kelly, and I really believe that he thought I was trying to pace Kelly using the motorbike.

We had just begun the Lissolo when an attack from Cornillet immediately put Rezze and Volpi out the back. The climb was packed to capacity with thousands of *tifosi*, and the cries for Ballerini reached a crescendo as the Italian took to the front in pursuit of the Frenchman. I shot off a few frames of Cornillet, as Kelly put on the pressure.

I stopped on the tip of the first summit, preferring to

Martial Gayant and Sean Kelly crest the summit of the Lissolo in 1991, watched by a phalanx of photographers and cameramen

A triumphant victory salute from Kelly – his third win in the Tour of Lombardy

take a roadside shot, as the race would surely reach its climax on such a steep ramp. I wasn't disappointed: one by one they came past, first Ballerini, then Sörensen, then Cornillet – each of these men simply blasted off the pace by Kelly's burst of speed near to the top. Only Gayant had resisted Kelly's attack, and Patrice soon had me right behind these two as we moved on to the easier, second part of the climb. We swiftly got past the three pursuers, deftly negotiated a tricky right-hand corner at high speed on the small dip, and were then attempting to squeeze past the two leaders as they raced onto the final ascent in the race.

Patrice was in brilliant form, and ignored all the warnings from the officials not to pass. Into the final few hundred metres, he elbowed his way past the RAI television motorbike to put me directly ahead of Gayant and Kelly as our envious colleagues looked on from behind. I got the pictures I most wanted of this great classic, with the two leaders' importance enhanced by

the impressive entourage of motorbikes, cars and television cameras.

Despite their attack, Gayant and Kelly only had 35 seconds in hand as they sped down the descent, reaching the main road to Monza with an even smaller advantage. Only 32 kilometres remained. But I clung to the conviction that Kelly would win, and sought to get some final shots of his glory day before it was time to head for the finish.

Patrice took me back once more, with just over ten kilometres to the finish now. But just as we were manoeuvring ourselves for one last stint at the side of Kelly's straining form, Torriani's car suddenly screamed away from its place just ahead of the leaders, and headed straight for us. The car was almost rubbing its bumper against our rear mudguard, so keen was its driver to move us on. Yet still Patrice didn't budge – this form of intimidation had long since failed to have any effect on either of us. We thought that, like always, Torriani

*'Gibi' Baronchelli scored a dubious victory in 1986, amid
speculation that the race-victory had been bought for him*

would be forced to pull away, as we ourselves continued
to pull back closer to the leaders. But this time the
Italian was at the very limits of his endurance with us,
and suddenly appeared alongside, yelling and
screaming for all his worth. I smiled teasingly at him,
slightly mystified as to why he was getting so excited
when we were doing no harm. But then a face appeared
out of the back window that scared the living daylights
out of me – it was Francesco Moser.

Together, the two legends of Italian cycling hurled
unparalleled abuse at me and Patrice. 'Basta! Basta!'
they cried. Now Torriani I can take with a pinch of salt,
even a smattering of arrogance; Moser I cannot. I'd
never seen my former hero so distressed, his dignified
features screwed up in anger and rage; I ashamedly
instructed Patrice to get us out of there quicker than
quickly. On our way to the finish, Jacques Garcia
explained why Torriani and Moser had lost their rag:
they were hoping desperately that Ballerini would close
the small gap and win this Giro di Lombardia. My

presence, so close to Kelly, appeared to them to be
jeopardising their hopes.

I slid gratefully off the motorbike at the finish,
grateful and satisfied after a good day's work in Italy –
my favourite hunting ground. I didn't really care about
Moser or Torriani: if they couldn't accept a foreigner
winning in Italy, that was their problem. When Kelly
cruised across the finish line a few minutes later, his
arms raised triumphantly high, I had a smile a mile wide
etched across my face. I felt an overwhelming burst of
emotion that Kelly had come good at the end of a
traumatic season, and towards the end of a glorious
career. If he were never to win a classic again, I knew I
would always cherish that day in Lombardy – cherish
the day when Kelly pulled back the years to remind us
all of his status in the history of cycling, and to kindle
the hope that this romantic classic will one day find a
more dignified stage from which to perform. The Giro di
Lombardia deserves at least that.

MORENO ARGENTIN

17 April 1991: Flèche Wallonne

It seemed a strange time to go it alone, with more than 70 kilometres, and two more ascents of the fearful Mur de Huy still to come. And they'd just started the sharp climb of Ben-Ahin which would be an even harder obstacle when it was attacked for a second time one hour later! But alone is how Moreno Argentin rode as he pounded away up the four-kilometre hill, leaving in his wake a confused, yet elite, group of men who had come together after an earlier attack by Dimitri Konychev, Frans Maassen and Johan Bruyneel had been nullified. Argentin's attack seemed of lesser significance than it eventually turned out to be. I shot a few obligatory frames – just for the record – expecting his accelerations to be parried by some of the men watching curiously as the Italian pulled away.

It was Claude Criquielion who took up the chase, suddenly fearful that Argentin was about to make them all work extremely hard in what was supposed to be a preparation race for next Sunday's Liège–Bastogne–Liège. The Belgian champion surged up the hill, giving his ever

familiar glance over his shoulder to those he hoped might follow. Two men did at first – Konychev and Jean-François Bernard – but they were still losing ground to Criquielion as the climb levelled out, while Criquielion himself was faring no better against the ruthless Italian. Even with only five kilometres of Argentin's attack completed, Criquielion's face portrayed a growing anxiety that he'd lost his quarry.

Argentin powered on ahead, now descending the leafy hillside towards the main road that led to Huy, whilst behind, his spreadeagled pursuers looked anxiously at each other. The thousands of people lining the 22-percent slope of the Mur de Huy couldn't fathom Argentin's strategy in what he was attempting now with 25 seconds' advantage. I was confused too, but grew more appreciative of the leader's motives after I'd photographed his chasers' desperate efforts on the rolling roads beyond the climb. Argentin had to be moving to withstand this chase! His style is deceptive, his face completely inscrutable, and it was therefore hard to gauge the exact scale of Argentin's effort.

Despite the ferocity of their four-up pursuit after Huy, the chasers were more than one-and-a-half minutes down as Argentin tackled the Côte d'Ereffe with 34 kilometres remaining. I'd waited there to photograph his chasers' efforts. Criquielion's face portrayed a desolate embarrassment at what Argentin was doing to him in his own country. Argentin had run amok in the heart of the Ardennes; he'd made fools of his rivals. He'd lent his own reputation to resurrect that of this popular classic, and he'd done it with no apparent discomfort to himself. That was the puzzling thing: how hard had he tried? I'd deliberately got in close on the final climb of Ben-Ahin, taking all the time in the world both to photograph and to study the Italian's expressions. But there were none – only a controlled power suppressed like that of a volcano within this human cannonball. Even before Argentin had crossed the finish line at Huy, I felt I'd seen the most brilliant individual performance by a cyclist in my time, certainly in a one-day classic. And when he did cross the line, half of Belgium was forced to agree: they hadn't seen anything quite like Moreno Argentin since the days of Eddy Merckx.

MIGUEL INDURAIN

11 August 1990: Clasicá San Sebastian

Through crowds three deep the two men raced to the very limit of their capabilities, each of them consciously aware of their popularity amongst the Basque spectators that cheered them along. They were climbing the Alto de Jaizkibel, a torturous eight-kilometre ascent at the end of a long hot day in Guipuzcoa, the easternmost province of the Basque country. For Miguel Indurain this final climb represented the final barrier to his first victory in the Clasicá San Sebastian. Still fresh from his brilliant stage win over Greg LeMond in the previous month's Tour de France, the handsome Pamplonan knew all about his adversary who was currently pushing up the pace. Marino Lejarreta, the hero of the Basques, had won this event three times already, and wasn't about to hand over 'his' race to Indurain, no matter how much he wanted it.

It was a moving sight for any cycling fan – these two conquistadors riding provocatively on the steepest part of the climb. For the past two kilometres Lejarreta had led, using his natural climbing skills to draw him and his shadow away from the tiring peloton. He seemed to enjoy the fact that only Indurain was left – a mark of Lejaretta's strengths even at the age of 33. And for a while his persecution had the heavier man in difficulty as they approached the most densely populated sections.

Then it was Indurain's turn to respond, inspired perhaps by the cheering crowds, or by the levelling road up ahead. Slowly but surely, the Banesto rider drew alongside Lejarreta, deliberately prolonging his presence as the terrain turned in his favour.

A glance over his left shoulder, a quick calculation of the road ahead, a rapid flick of the gear lever, and he was suddenly gone. His long powerful legs churned the big gear so effortlessly, while behind Lejarreta slipped rapidly out of sight, soon to be gobbled up by the chasing group slowly forming in the wake of Indurain's spectacular escape. The climb went on, the initial flat that had helped Indurain now replaced by a growing steepness that forced the 26-year-old out of the saddle to parry this threat. But there was no threat – not really, not to a man destined for greatness far beyond this. Indurain powered on, heading confidently towards the descent that seemed certain to take him into San Sebastian as winner.

Indurain passed the summit of the Jaizkibel with already 30 seconds' advantage, and with a 34-kilometre descent still to come. Already on his big chainring for the last two kilometres, Indurain had only to slip into his smallest cog to up the pace even more. As he negotiated the difficult corkscrew descent above the Bay of Biscay he had no time to enjoy the view – no time to consider the surroundings as he plunged down, down. On reaching the main road he had pushed his lead to one-minute or more, with 25 kilometres still left; and by Orayzun he'd gained nearly two minutes; there was no stopping the man, no denying him his success. His immense physique bounded into view down the long sunlit Almeda del Boulevard, his arrival greeted with the fervour normally reserved for kings. Indurain had arrived – the prince of cycling was one step nearer his ascendancy.

The Grand Prix des Nations was traditionally a late-season battleground for time triallists like Laurent Fignon, seen here on his way to course-record and victory in the 1989 race in Cannes

STILL A CLASSIC

When is a classic not a classic? If the officers of the Fédération Internationale de Cyclisme Professionel (FICP) are to be believed, it is when they decree as such, and not, sadly, when history is telling the world something else. The political and structural shake-up within the professional sport in recent years has drastically altered the face of cycling. Amongst other things, a synthetic prominence has been placed on new races such as England's Wincanton Classic, Canada's Grand Prix de Montréal, and the Netherlands' Grand Prix de la Liberation. To make way for these modern 'classics', and to ensure the public and media appeal of the recently formed World Cup competition, a handful of hitherto sacred races have seen their status devalued by the FICP to the point where they are fighting for their very existence in the light of the pressure to commercialise the classics.

The real classics derive their strength and identity from their different national and cultural roots, yet the 'mondialisation' of the sport, which has provided its new adherents, threatens the very races that once inspired its creation. Races such as the Omloop Het Volk, Ghent–Wevelgem and Flèche Wallonne – all of them Belgian – have for years played an important role in the imagery of the classics, at the same time achieving immense notoriety because of their specific 'attractions' for both cyclist and fan. On a visit to the Omloop Het Volk in early March, one can hardly fail to be impressed by the courage and bravado of cyclists tackling wet or icy cobbled climbs so early in the season, or of the efforts of an Etienne De Wilde or Ronny Van Holen in winning the city of Ghent's famous race – for to win in the Omloop as a native Gentenaar can be the highlight of a top professional's career.

The history of races like the Omloop Het Volk is almost as long as that of many of the 'monuments' featured in this book, and they take a corresponding share of the glory. To a photographer, these sacred races have for years been an eternal source of inspiration, and this book wouldn't be complete without at least some reference to them. For so much of my own satisfaction has been drawn from photographing races such as Het Volk, Ghent–Wevelgem and Flèche Wallonne where, away from the stifling clamour and hype of the big classics, a refreshing air of intimacy is to be enjoyed. Het Volk serves as an exciting opening clash for the new season, while at the same time pointing the way to the 'big' classics one month later – while Ghent–Wevelgem provides a great midweek scrap between the ardour of the Tour of Flanders and the foreboding of Paris–Roubaix. In wet weather its famous double ascent of the Kemmelberg is one of the true highlights of the season.

The Flèche Wallonne's *raison d'être* is obvious. Coming as it does just four days before Liège–Bastogne–Liège, this hilly event acts as a purposeful preparation event for those *rouleurs* wishing to succeed in *La Doyenne*. Even then, one cannot fail to appreciate Flèche Wallonne's impressive history dating back to 1936. Originally this event was considered as important as its big sister, and the two races took it in turns to be held first – initially on successive days, then more recently with a gap of at least three days. In those earlier days the two races enjoyed the collective title of 'Weekend Ardennais', and it became a most difficult yet sought-after distinction to win both races on the same weekend. The most impressive classic victory I've ever seen was the 1991 Flèche Wallonne, when Moreno Argentin rode away from his opponents with over 70 kilometres still to go, building a winning advantage of more than two minutes as he crossed the summit of the Mur de Huy for the fourth and final time.

A few days later, when Argentin won Liège–Bastogne–Liège as well, he unwittingly resurrected the popular appeal of Flèche Wallonne by becoming the first man since Eddy Merckx in 1972 to win the 'Ardennais Double'. The Italian's feat highlighted the status of events such as Flèche Wallonne compared to their big brothers and sisters. It also highlighted the sport's administrators attempts to undermine such races.

The Kemmelberg in the wet; panting riders emerge through clouds of their own steam in the 1988 Ghent–Wevelgem

Other events such as the Netherlands' Amstel Gold, the Basque Country's Clasicá San Sebastian, Switzerland's Championship of Zurich, and even Paris–Tours, play a part in the imagery of the classics, only to a much lesser degree; but they were all considered worthy classics before the onset of the world cup. The interest at these events centres as much on each country's style of hosting a one-day race as it does on the racing itself. The style varies from the austere, polite appreciation of a Swiss audience, to the drunken rowdiness of the less desirable Dutch fans, the sophisticated, yet often wild manner of the Basques, and the complete indifference of a French nation that hasn't won its second-biggest classic in 35 years.

Presented as they are, the new 'classics' simply cannot be appreciated in the same light as their

The Amstel Gold is traditionally an all-Dutch affair 1988
Champion of Holland Adrie Van Der Poel leads a PDM group in
pursuit of winner Jelle Nijdam

Phil Anderson spins out the thread-like peloton followed by Eric
Vanderaerden in the 1984 Het Volk.

grandfathers, nor even in the same breath it takes to mention their name. There's something about a classic that sets it apart from any other race. It is not something that one can designate simply by using the word in some attention-grabbing title, which can after all be created out of nothing. A classic means just that: an ageless, enduring, immortal thing – not an event staged purely for television, or for short-term gain on the part of some politician or sponsor. Yet this is what the FICP is allowing to happen.

The 60-year-old Grand Prix des Nations time trial is another sad example of the way the sport is heading under the present regime. Until recently, it stood alone as one of the most forbidding races in the calendar, but its organisers have now caused it to lose its distinction by naively letting it be swallowed up amidst the fast-moving ambitions of the World Cup competition.

To a photographer the new races offer little in the way of dramatic images anyway – and that must say a lot about an event's future prospects. The established classics have a lot to offer, partly by nature of their heritage, partly by nature of the courses they are raced over. Their longevity has been built around familiar landmarks, where an incident made famous there one year will be readily recalled ten years later, and by linking towns and cities along the way so that the race belongs as much to the people as it does to a sponsor. Penetrate any likely looking group of spectators on the centuries-old cobblestones of the Oude Kwaremont in Flanders, and one could easily be present at any number of classics or semi-classics – Het Volk and the Tour of Flanders, to name but two. But try doing the same with the suburban delights of the Mount Royal climb in Montreal, the mid-town claustrophobia of Eindhoven, or the anonymity of Wilson's Avenue in Brighton!

Only time will tell if the FICP has found the right formula in taking professional cycling to a worldwide audience, or whether it has succeeded in destroying those events that have played such a vital role in the development of the sport's identity. The blood, sweat

125

The Clasicá San Sebastian has gained prominence thanks to the achievements of men like Marino Lejarreta and Miguel Indurain, seen here attacking the Alto Jaizkibel in 1990

*The only Frenchman to make the podium of the Paris–Tours since
1956 is the winner of that year's race Albert Bouvet! Now he is
the technical director of the race, seen here kissing a hostess after
the 1991 event*

and tears that have been shed by champions past and
present in making the classics what they are today
should not be forgotten or diluted. There are qualities
you cannot measure when talking of tradition, of
achievement, of courage – and the established classics
that include Het Volk, Ghent–Wevelgem and Flèche
Wallonne base their attractions on such values. Nobody
can deny the success of the new races, if that is their
destiny anyway. But if that comes at the expense of
races that have played such an important role within the
sport, then there's something very wrong.

Events such as the Wincanton Classic and the Grand

Prix de Montréal, slickly organised as they are, have
little purpose in the traditional world of cycling, based
as it is in continental Europe, beyond their materialistic
value, and as such will never attain the glorious sense
of tradition that enabled so many of the true classics to
grow into what they are today. Races like Ghent–
Wevelgem must always be there, as must the Grand
Prix des Nations. And they must be there long after the
politicians have found some other gimmick to amuse
themselves with. As a well-written colleague of mine
once wrote, 'These classic races are the cornerstones of
professional cycling – and always will be.'

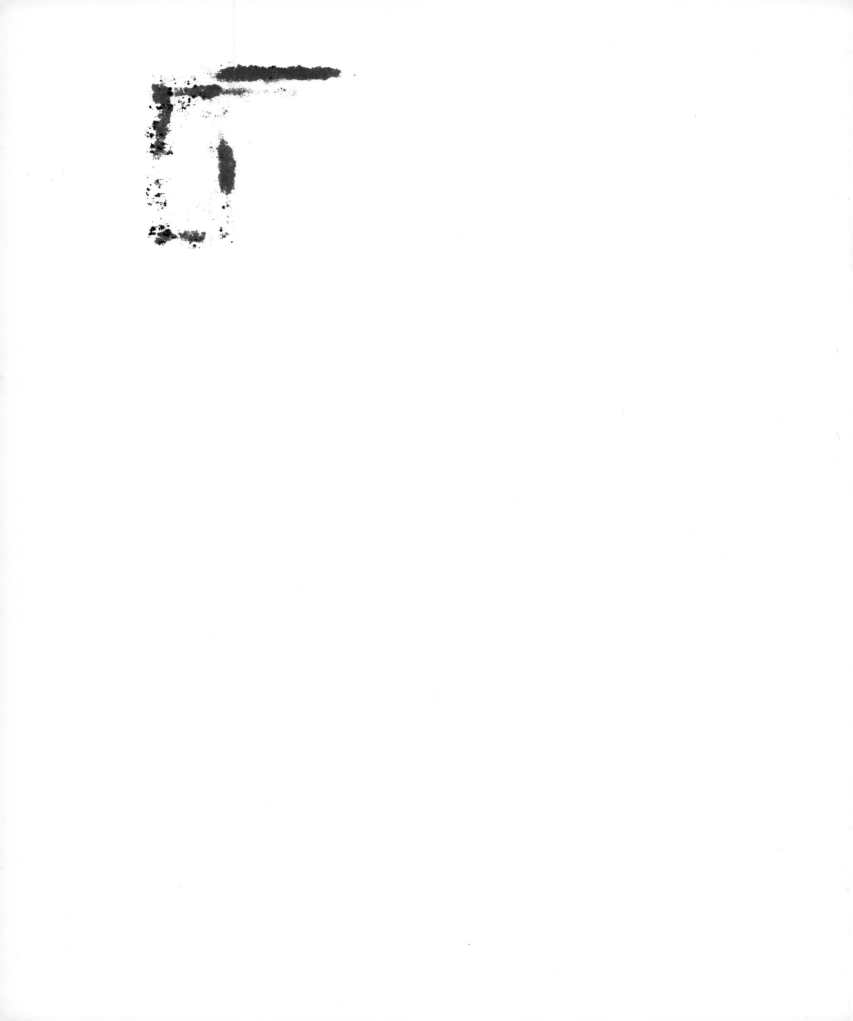

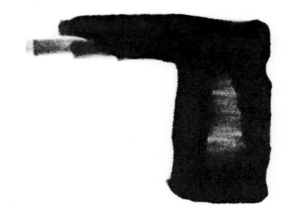

4y   13/06/05